W. Somerset Maugham

A CANDID PORTRAIT

W. Somerset Maugham

A CANDID PORTRAIT

BY KARL G. PFEIFFER

Introduction by Jerome Weidman

New York · W · W · NORTON & COMPANY · INC ·

Contents

Introduction

By JEROME WEIDMAN

THEY USED to tell a story when I was a boy about Alice Roosevelt Longworth, the witty daughter of our twenty-sixth President, who was for many years one of the most popular hostesses in the nation's capital. On an occasion the more important details of which are now vague in my mind, Mrs. Longworth was asked by her father to entertain a Middle Western businessman who had been summoned to Washington by the redoubtable TR because the man's eminence in the leather industry had suddenly made him a key figure in one of the President's plans for the nation's economic welfare. At the dinner party she gave in his honor, Mrs. Longworth seated the leather tycoon on her right, where he could be subjected at close range to the charm that had in its time, and in the service of the republic, melted everything from British iciness to Japanese inscrutability.

Like any seasoned general opening a battle in the

classic manner, Mrs. Longworth inquired with the soup if her guest was interested in the opera. No, said the leather tycoon politely, and that was all he did say. Somewhat taken aback by this unaccustomed curtness, Mrs. Longworth was silent for several minutes. Then, rallying her forces, she asked with a friendly smile as the fish was served if her guest cared for the theatre. No, said the guest, and seemed content to let the remark stand without further expansion. Metaphorically tightening her belt for the next round, Mrs. Longworth inquired with the roast if her guest had read a new novel that was the talk of the literary world. No, said the leather merchant as politely as before, and became absorbed by the food on his plate.

His absorption was not, however, total. As he cut his meat he apparently noted out of the corner of his eye a slight touch of desperation on the face of the woman who had never before been at a loss for a subject of conversation with a guest.

"Mrs. Longworth," the leather king said with a kindly twinkle in his eye as he leaned toward the famous hostess, "may I suggest that you try me on leather?"

She did, and for the rest of the evening Mrs. Longworth couldn't get a word in edgewise.

It is not quite accurate to say that I had a similar experience during my first meeting with Karl Pfeiffer, but whenever I think of that initial encounter, the story of Mrs. Longworth and the leather merchant does come to mind.

Mr. Pfeiffer, who lives in the Connecticut commuting

town that I call home, is a Professor of English at New York University where, in addition to his more formal duties, he keeps a paternal eye on the Book Club, an organization devoted to the dubious proposition that a student's knowledge of the language employed by Shakespeare and Swift will be enhanced if once a month he is allowed to listen to a few remarks by a professional writer. Not because the supply of professional writers is limited, but because it is a tradition with most of them to profess an intense dislike for public speaking, Mr. Pfeiffer's task is not a simple one. He is, however, a conscientious man and, more important, a practical one: when beef is unavailable he—or rather his students— will dine on radish tops. One day, therefore, he rang me up and, after introducing himself, asked if I would address his Book Club. Being a professional writer, I do not like to slight any of the traditions of my craft, and so I made all the traditional protests about detesting public speaking. Being an alumnus of New York University, however, I then allowed myself to be persuaded to yield with reluctance. A date was set and, since Mr. Pfeiffer and I had never clapped eyes on one another, he very sensibly suggested that we meet at the local railroad station for the ride into New York.

As several thousand commuters can and do testify, it is not a memorable journey even under the best circumstances, and the best circumstances rarely occur in the mid-afternoon, when Mr. Pfeiffer and I rode in together: it is the time of day when our railroad, having strained its Coolidge-era rolling stock by getting the commuters to town in the morning, gives the cars a rest against the evening task of getting the commuters back home, and so trots out its museum pieces for casual afternoon travelers.

There was nothing casual about Mr. Pfeiffer and myself. Like any two people who have met for the first time without the cushioning services of an intermediary, neither of us could think of anything to say. As the train pulled out of our station, Mr. Pfeiffer asked a trifle nervously if I was working on a new book. No, I said, and since there is nothing any writer can add to this dismal confession, I added nothing. The train stopped at the first station. Mr. Pfeiffer, clearly thinking hard, stared out the window. When the train started he smiled hopefully and asked if I had read any good books lately. Since the writer who, while having trouble with his own work, is capable of making glowing remarks about his contemporaries has yet to be born, I naturally said no and let it go at that. Mr. Pfeiffer couldn't. He was, after all, my host. Somewhat desperately, as we pulled into the next station, he asked if I liked the work of X, a highly successful poet. Since I didn't, and had said so often, this hardly seemed the moment to reverse my position, so I said no. Mr. Pfeiffer, who was now breathing hard, waited until we pulled into and out of the next station before asking if I had read the newest book by Y, a prolific composer of historical romances. I have no very strong feelings about historical romances, but I am a slow reader and had not yet finished Y's previous book, so again I was forced to say no. Seeing the look in Mr. Pfeiffer's eye, where desperation was beginning to give

INTRODUCTION

way to what seemed to me perfectly justifiable notions about homicide, I cleared my throat and said, "Why don't you try me on Maugham?"

It is at this point that my experience parts company with that of Mrs. Longworth. She took the leather tycoon at his word and, as I have noted, she thereupon had trouble getting one of her own in edgewise. Mr. Pfeiffer, on the other hand, instead of taking me at my word, lit up like a coronation chandelier and, instead of trying me on Maugham, started telling me about him.

It turned out that he had known Mr. Maugham for many years and, like most people who have had this happy experience, Mr. Pfeiffer had a good deal to say about it. So did I because, by one of those coincidences that a novelist would not dare use in his work, I too had known Mr. Maugham and, naturally, I too had a good deal to say about it.

Unlike Mrs. Longworth, when I have something to say, I rarely find it difficult to get a word, or even a paragraph, in edgewise. Probably because Mr. Pfeiffer is a gentleman, this did not prove to be one of those rare occasions. I talked away for a while, and then Mr. Pfeiffer talked, and then it was my turn again, and then to our considerable surprise a conductor was standing in the aisle telling us somewhat tartly that the train had been standing in Grand Central for quite some time and when did we intend to get off?

We got off at once, but all the way down to N.Y.U. in the taxi we continued to talk about Mr. Maugham, and aside from a few interruptions for the consumption of food and the taking of holidays, we have been doing it ever since.

It is, I think, a comment on Mr. Maugham's personality that, in all the years of this marathon conversation, Mr. Pfeiffer and I have never repeated ourselves. Thus, I think, it must have been with those, for example, who had "seen Shelley plain" and later, on meeting one another, learned this exciting fact about themselves. Contact with greatness may not, if we are to believe the debunking school of biographers, always leave an indelible mark. It does, however, usually leave a subject for conversation.

It is not my place to assess Mr. Maugham's standing with posterity as a writer. I will say, however, that no matter how the votes go on artistic grounds, there is no doubt in my mind that his position will be high on the list for which the yardstick employed is character. Not because of his kindness and generosity, of which Mr. Maugham possesses a good deal more than he likes the world to know, but because he is what we used to call, when I was a law student, *sui generis*.

There are not many like him. There never have been. There probably never will be. Knowing him has been one of the more rewarding experiences of my life. I have a feeling that this is equally true of most people who have known him.

Reading what Mr. Pfeiffer has written helps to explain why.

W. Somerset Maugham

A CANDID PORTRAIT

CHAPTER 1

Maugham Changes His Mind

I HAD known W. Somerset Maugham for eighteen years when, one bright September afternoon in 1941, we sat opposite each other over a brandy in the drawing room of a house he had rented in Beverly Hills. I thought it quite a grand house but Maugham called it a funny little place which he had got at a bargain—seven hundred dollars a month—because it had only one swimming pool, and a rectangular one at that.

Maugham was dressed in gray slacks, a tweed jacket, and black moccasins, and he wore them with the upper-class Britisher's knack of making even new clothes appear faintly shabby and disreputable. Not that there was ever anything bohemian in Maugham's dress or manner. He always played the part of the reserved, well-to-do, top-drawer Englishman—a type he satirized mercilessly in his stories. Sometimes he wore a monocle.

Except that he is shorter than the photographs suggest, those taken late in life do him justice, perhaps because he refuses to allow them to be touched up. "I can understand a person of forty wanting to look younger than he is," he once remarked. "But when you're old, why not look as old as possible?" The deep lines around the eyes have been piously preserved in the photographs, as well as the bitter, disillusioned expression that is his trademark. His mouth is thin and turns down at the corners; the mustache is close-cropped and scrawny. His hair is rather long and brushed straight back, and his ears are large and naked. His bearing, except when he is relaxed, is military. He looks like a slightly shopworn Mephistopheles.

His daughter Liza—then Mrs. Vincent Paravicini, now Lady John Hope—was with us, for she was also visiting him at this time, and Gerald Haxton, Maugham's secretary for some twenty-five years. Liza had dined with Bette Davis the night before, and I asked her whether Bette realized that she got her start as an important actress by playing Mildred in Maugham's *Of Human Bondage.*

"She realizes," said Liza, "and she's grateful to Pa."

We chatted about the progress of the war, the progress of the script Maugham was working on, his dissatisfaction with the novel he had just finished (*The Hour Before the Dawn*). I mentioned a book about Maugham which had recently been published.

"What do you think of it, Willie?" I asked.

"I-I h-haven't r-read it, I-I never read an-anything about myself."

"I have," said Gerald Haxton. "It's awful. Don't trust a thing he says. He hasn't even got the name of Willie's grandfather right. That's the third book on Willie and they're all rotten."

"A professor wrote one and sent it to me asking me to write a foreword to it," Maugham added. "But as it purported to show that my stories are nothing but a poor imitation of Maupassant's, I refused."

Maugham seemed unaware that he was contradicting what he had just said, and none of us ventured to point this out to him. He sniffed his brandy and held it up to the light. "I hardly ever drink it. No liqueurs." He was sitting with one leg under him, saying little but somehow dominating the group. His restless and penetrating eyes somewhat belied the affability of his manner. You felt that the Maugham eyes were appraising you, and they were. He took no one at face value, and the Maugham appraisal seldom erred on the side of charity. He called his habit of cutting people down to size "coolness of scrutiny," and he thought he might have inherited it from his lawyer ancestors. What he said of Edmund Gosse was no doubt true of himself—that he took pleasure in observing men's absurdity. Yet you were not made uncomfortable by it, because his speech was courteous and his manners courtly. When you got to know him you realized that he considered everyone, including himself, a bit of a stinker. But then he rather liked stinkers.

Maugham shifted his position. Then he announced in a mock pontifical tone, "After my death, Dr. Pfeiffer will write the authoritative work on Maugham."

Amazed and embarrassed, I tried to find words to express gratitude, but Maugham cut me short. He likes you to be grateful to him, but he doesn't want to hear about it. Had he guessed it had long been my ambition to write a book about him some day? Had he decided to give the project his blessing, or was his remark a whim of the moment? Maugham appears to be a modest man, some think a cynical one; it doesn't upset him to discover that most people who know him want something from him. He doesn't hesitate to use others, and he expects others to use him—if they are smart enough to get away with it. He once told me that I was a fool if I didn't make some money out of knowing him for so many years.

From our first meeting I had made some notes of what he said, wore, ate, and looked like, but I had not done so openly. Sometimes, if he said something particularly good that I wanted to be sure to record accurately, I would slip out of the room—unobtrusively I thought—and jot it down. More often, when I was visiting him or had spent an evening with him, I would make notes before going to bed. Now I could take notes openly. I no longer had to try to steer the conversation around to a topic on which I wanted his opinion—a game as likely to deceive the observant Mr. Maugham as a psychic bid is likely to deceive his good friend Mr. Charles Goren. From that day, whenever I wanted enlightenment, I sat at the Master's knee, pad and pencil in hand, and asked questions.

Luckily, he didn't mind answering questions. He answered freely but not disingenuously. When he didn't want to answer, he flatly said so. He wasn't offended by a question, no matter how personal or unflattering its implications: we agreed that the more I knew, the better I could write. But he knew I was going to broadcast much of what he told me, and he wasn't so naive as to expect me to be more discreet than he had been. He was well aware that in these informal question-and-answer sessions he was sitting for his portrait, and unless he was in a mood to appear revolting, he wasn't above flattering the likeness a bit. When it came to facts, he was quite dependable. Occasionally his memory played tricks on him, particularly in the matter of dates, but he didn't lie. In matters of opinion he told me what he wanted me to believe—and tell others.

He was, for example, always perfectly charming in what he had to say about Americans. He said that Americans had given him most of his fame and fortune (true) and that he was very grateful to us (also true). He did once stigmatize as childish our faith in the notion that all redheads are passionate, but against that he had many splendid and complimentary things to say of our taste, especially the taste of our working classes. He spoke of going to an exhibition of modern French paintings in San Francisco. These would have meant nothing on Park Avenue, he said, but the Lockheed workers and their girls came and argued. It was obvious that the pictures meant something to them.

On another occasion he remarked that what particularly struck him about Americans is that if you give them the best, they will eat it up; but they won't touch the second-rate masquerading as first. When the WPA gave cheap concerts and the conductors padded their programs with second-rate works, the audiences received these coldly but were enthusiastic over Bach and Mozart.

"Not long ago," Maugham continued, "I edited an

anthology of modern English and American literature. I
gave the reader the best I knew, and much of it was
pretty difficult. Yet it sold in the hundred thousands in the
United States."

All this was very pleasant to hear, but I put much of it
down to my being an American, Maugham's good manners, and his wish to have the record stand thus. For his
manners are impeccable; he is never unintentionally rude.
He meant everything he said, but he wasn't expressing
his whole opinion of us. To an American he would say
only what he liked about Americans. Once Maugham was
offered a large sum to write three essays on Britain,
France, and the United States. He refused the offer.
"Where would I live if I wrote them?" he asked. Although
I enjoyed hearing this Britisher praise us, I found it difficult to believe that the man who was so caustic about his
own countrymen would always spare us. The publication
of *A Writer's Notebook* in 1949 showed that he hadn't.

A few months after the Beverly Hills meeting I was in
New York, and I told my agent that Maugham had suggested I write a book about him.

"Get it in writing," my agent said.

Maugham happened to be in New York at that time,
and although I was dining with him that night I sat down
and wrote him a letter, asking him to put the permission
in writing. A few days later I had his answer. He didn't
mention that the suggestion had originated with him, but
he told me to go ahead if I wanted to. He should warn
me, however, that a couple of other chaps had the same
idea and were, in fact, just waiting for him to die to bring

out their books. He didn't say who the chaps were, and years later when I reminded him of them he replied that he didn't think either work amounted to much.

Ten years later Maugham did an about-face. He is a reticent man, and he may have been shocked by the frankness of several biographies of writers that appeared about that time. At any rate he announced that he didn't want a Somerset Maugham biography. He wrote me that Sam Behrman and several other top-flight professionals wanted to do the job, and since he had refused to help them, he must refuse to help me. He wrote as if the matter were being discussed for the first time. He had made up his mind to do everything in his power to discourage a Maugham biography. He thereupon instructed his literary executor to refuse all aid and comfort to the enemy who might undertake to write his life. He knew he couldn't prevent anyone from writing a biography, but by withholding materials he could guarantee that it would be a poor one. It was his notion that a poor biography wouldn't be widely read. A number of people who thought differently failed to change his mind.

This book, then, is not a biography of Maugham, and it is certainly not the "authoritative" work which in 1941 Maugham suggested that I write. Although, in order to tell a coherent story, I have arranged my material chronologically and have drawn upon printed sources to fill in gaps where I had no first-hand knowledge, the book is just what the title implies—a candid portrait of Somerset Maugham. It sketches his life; it has something to say of his writing, especially in regard to the use he made of his own personality in drawing his characters. Once he re-marked that no writer could draw a convincing character solely from observation; he had to have some of that char-acter in himself if he were to make him live for the reader. A large number of Maugham's characters are aspects of himself. None of them, not even Philip Carey or the first-person narrator of so many of the short stories and novels, is a complete self-portrait; they are all less complex and more consistent than he. But many of them show some-thing of him. With sardonic humor he has made most of these characters unpleasant, men respected but disliked by their fictional associates.

I plan to take the reader behind the scenes, a danger-ous thing to do, Maugham said, for people are easily dis-illusioned, and by lowering the mask you destroy the illusion. Then they are angry with you, for it was the illu-sion they loved. But Maugham also said he wanted no one to think better of him than he deserves. At present, very few do.

Reading over the book I have written, I wonder if I have not unwittingly given the impression that I know Maugham better than I do. I refer to so many visits with him that it sounds as if I were constantly at his elbow. I wasn't. There were long intervals when I neither saw nor heard from him. A number of persons saw him more fre-quently than I did, though few now living have known him longer—thirty-five years. We never lived in the same place, and I seldom saw him for more than a week at a time. But he was a great traveler and I got around a bit, and not infrequently our paths crossed. I visited him in various places—France, California, South Carolina, New York. We exchanged a good many letters.

When we were together I made notes on what he said; when we separated I wrote down all I could remember. I will not swear that the words I have put into his mouth were always, word for word, his. But I am certain that I have not foisted on him any opinions which he did not express at one time or another, however different the opinion may be from those expressed to others on the same subject—or to me at other times.

If others who know him write about him, they may present a quite different Maugham. For he is a number of people. I doubt that any friend, no matter how close or constant in attendance, knows all sides of his many-sided nature. He is abnormally reticent, he likes to appear remote and mysterious, and his stammer effectively stifles whatever rare impulses he may have to talk about himself.

As he himself once remarked, only God sees a human being exactly as he is. The rest of us see others through the medium of our own personalities, and we are naive if we imagine that we understand another person completely, regardless of our opportunities for observation. We can test the truth of this remark by comparing Maugham's sketch of Arnold Bennett with Frank Swinnerton's. Two trained and acute observers have given us two Arnold Bennetts who have little if anything in common. Although my memory of what Maugham said and did in my presence is good, another person may perhaps have seen and remembered other things, and thus sketch a different portrait.

Maugham also remarked that very few people really know him, and those few not nearly so well as they think they do. I quite agree.

CHAPTER 2

The Lean Years (1874-1907)

WHEN W. Somerset Maugham was born on January 25, 1874, the English literary giants were a very different breed from those who were to rule the roost as his contemporaries. In 1874, George Eliot and Carlyle were still writing; Tennyson and Browning were at the height of their fame; Matthew Arnold had recently published "Culture and Anarchy" and Walter Pater his essay on Wordsworth; Ruskin had twenty-six years ahead of him to lead England into the paths of culture and righteousness; and Victoria's reign had another twenty-seven years to go.

Britisher though he is, Maugham was born in Paris, where his father was solicitor to the British Embassy. The family lived in an apartment on the Avenue d'Antin. The Maughams were substantial people; for over a hundred years the male Maughams had practiced law. The novelist was always proud of the fact that his grandfather had been one of the two founders of the Incorporated Law Society and is written up in the *Dictionary of National Biography*. Maugham's father was a great traveler, as the son was to be. He had been to Turkey, Greece, and Asia Minor, and the apartment was filled with Tanagra statuettes, Rhodes ware, Turkish daggers, and other souvenirs of travel. He also had a large library of travel books. Once he brought back from Morocco a sign against the Evil Eye, a device Maugham now uses as a kind of monogram. It appears on the covers of all his books; it can also be seen over the entrance to his home in France, on the matchboxes in his drawing room, and in other unlikely places. Few people know exactly what it is, but almost everybody identifies it with Maugham.

Christened "William Somerset," the boy was called "Willie," and "Willie" he has remained to his friends all his life. Only once was he addressed as "Somerset." The speaker was a spirit at a seance, and the error did nothing to dispel Willie's skepticism regarding spiritualism and the spiritual life.

Maugham's father, whom the son fancied he resembled, was extremely ugly; his mother, who was twenty years younger than her husband, was very beautiful. They were known in their circle as Beauty and the Beast. Their circle included the best people, titled folk for whom adultery seems to have been routine social behavior. The son dearly loved his mother, but filial love did not preclude intellectual curiosity. How, Maugham wondered, could his lovely, much-sought-after mother remain faithful to that ugly little man she was married to? Maugham concluded that she did so remain, but he seems to have regarded her chastity as quixotic in the extreme.

For many years Maugham's mother suffered from tuberculosis, and Maugham remembers the string of donkeys that stopped at the door to provide her with asses' milk, believed then to be good for women suffering from that disease. The doctors of the day also had a quaint notion that having a child was efficacious for the female tubercular. Mrs. Maugham's case should have undermined the theory, for after having six sons she died when she was only thirty-eight. Willie was eight at the time.

Willie has very little recollection of his mother, but he vividly recalls an event that took place shortly before her death. Although she had borne many children, Mrs. Maugham seems to have had a premonition that she would not survive the confinement she expected in a few weeks, and she was unhappy that her sons when they grew up would not know what she had looked like. The only photograph of herself had been taken almost twenty years before. One day when her husband was out she called her maid, had herself dressed in an evening gown of white satin, made her desperate way to a photographer's, was photographed, and struggled home, collapsing on the doorstep.

Whatever he put into his books Maugham usually forgot as soon as he had read the proofs. This incident, which he used in two books, I once heard him tell to dinner guests in his home. The passage of sixty years had not dimmed its poignancy for him. The photograph of his mother still stands on his bedside table.

Two years after his mother's death, Maugham's father died, just after he had built and furnished a summer house outside Paris. It was decided to send Willie to

England to live with an uncle, Henry Maugham, vicar of Whitstable in Kent, the Reverend William Carey of *Of Human Bondage*. In preparation for living in England, Willie was taken out of the French school he had been attending and taught English by an English clergyman attached to the British Embassy. His lessons consisted of reading aloud the police-court news, and there are those who believe that these lessons left their mark on Willie's fiction.

As everybody knows, *Of Human Bondage* is based on Maugham's youth and early manhood, but it is a novel, not an autobiography, and therefore not always reliable as to the facts of Maugham's life, for the novelist made such changes as were necessary to translate fact into good fiction. There is, for example, no mention of the eight formative years in France. Philip Carey's early years are spent in England, and he is completely English. He is an only child; his mother dies after his father; he has a club foot. Whitstable becomes Blackstable in the novel; and Canterbury, where Willie went to school, becomes Tercanbury.

Nevertheless, the early chapters of the novel are much closer to fact than the later ones. Those describing life at the vicarage are almost straight autobiography. When he was an old man Maugham read these chapters aloud to make a phonograph record for the blind. He had not looked at the novel since he had corrected the proofs. When he started to read the words he had written some forty years before, the unhappy memories of his childhood in Whitstable came flooding back, and to his intense

THE LEAN YEARS (1874–1907)

mortification Maugham burst into tears and had to discontinue the reading.

Most of the characters in the novel differ markedly from their prototypes. Once Maugham remarked, "I could name the original of every character in the novel, but I wouldn't. They were all altered for the purposes of fiction, and it wouldn't be fair to identify the originals." (He has, however, identified a few.) The two who suffered the least change are undoubtedly the Reverend Henry Maugham and his wife, Willie's uncle and aunt, for in the two other books in which they appear—one of them non-fiction—they are exactly like the Reverend William Carey and his wife. But perhaps even these are not faithful copies of the originals. They are his uncle and aunt as the forty-year-old author of *Of Human Bondage* conceived them to be. But thirty-five years later, when Maugham edited his notebooks for publication, he concluded that Uncle Henry had an elfin, tongue-in-cheek humor conspicuously lacking in the Vicar of the novel.

Once, trying to separate fact from fiction in *Of Human Bondage*, I asked Maugham whether it was fair to say that the thoughts and emotions of Philip at a given time were his at that age, and he agreed that it was. He added that many of Philip's experiences were his; others happened to people he knew and he transferred them to Philip; some were imaginary. Clearly, then, although many of the facts of Maugham's life are there, the novel is not the place to go for facts one can swear by.

Willie spent the next half-dozen years in and near Whitstable. His was the stereotyped unhappy childhood of many novels—the high-strung, unloved, frustrated orphan boy thrust into an unsympathetic environment where adults are well-meaning but stupid, schoolmates boorish, schoolmasters tyrannical—except one, an idealist scorned by his colleagues. This good man introduces the lonely boy to the world of books, the real world of beauty and truth and goodness.

If this sounds like a lot of other novels, we should bear in mind that this is only a small part of *Of Human Bondage*. The novel was written before miserable childhoods became standard literary equipment for sensitive little boys, and it remains one of the finest treatments of a now-hackneyed theme, partly because Maugham has a horror of emotional excess and Philip's sufferings are muted.

Muted though they are, Philip's sufferings are deep and real, for he has a club foot, a minor physical handicap which wrought major emotional havoc in the boy's life. Similarly, all his life Maugham has been afflicted with a stammer. He is disinclined to talk about it, and not until 1938 did he bring himself to refer to it in print, but in an oblique way he made painfully clear its tragic impact on his life. In 1933, in an essay on his friend Arnold Bennett, Maugham wrote: "Everybody knows that Arnold was afflicted with a very bad stammer; it was painful to watch the struggle he had sometimes to get the words out. It was torture to him. Few realised the exhaustion it caused him to speak. What to most men was as easy as breathing, to him was a constant strain. It tore his nerves to pieces. Few knew the humiliations it exposed him to, the ridicule it excited in many, the impatience it aroused, the awkwardness of feeling that made some people find him tiresome; and the minor exasperation of thinking of a good, amusing or apt remark and not venturing to say it in case the stammer ruined it. Few knew the distressing sense it gave rise to of a bar to complete contact with other men. It may be that except for the stammer which forced him to introspection Arnold would never have become a writer."

When he was thirteen, Willie was sent to King's School in Canterbury, a few miles from Whitstable. His unhappy life in this medieval institution of learning is described movingly in *Of Human Bondage*. Three years later his schooling was interrupted by a lung infection, and his uncle, knowing that Willie's mother and aunt had suffered from tuberculosis, sent him to the south of France for nine months.

When he returned to King's School, Willie was faced with the problem of choosing a profession to prepare for, a problem complicated on the one hand by his stammer, on the other by his uncle's notion that there were only a few professions in which a gentleman might properly engage. Someone suggested the Civil Service, and Uncle Henry wrote a friend in the Home Office for advice. The friend replied that since entrance to the service was now determined on the basis of competitive examination, the wrong class of persons had got into it, and the Civil Service was no longer a fit profession for a gentleman. That, Willie says, settled that. He himself had always wanted to be a writer, but it was hopeless to urge this— writing wasn't a gentleman's profession either. The law was out, since a stammerer could never become a barrister. Willie thought there had been enough lawyers in the family anyway. Despite the stammer and a lack of vocation amounting to aversion, Uncle Henry decided that the boy should prepare for the ministry, and at thirteen, the boy was unable to rebel successfully.

Beneath his conventional exterior Maugham has always been something of a rebel, though few who know him realize it. A certain native caution linked with a sense of what is fitting dissuaded him from flamboyant acts of rebellion until he could well afford them. The first fruit of his rebelliousness was a year in Heidelberg, where he went when he was seventeen. He escaped vicarage life, Maugham says, because he was spending his own money and his uncle wanted to get rid of him. His uncle didn't like him very much, but Maugham doesn't blame him. He says he wasn't a likable boy.

Heidelberg was Willie's first step towards self-realization. At seventeen, self-realization did not include riotous living. For several years the boy remained a timid but determined observer of the seamy side of life. He saw sex from the sidelines, fascinated and a little horrified. And, if the truth be told, all his life Maugham has been too fastidious in taste, too squeamish in stomach to indulge excessively in the vices which his tolerant mind condones. In Heidelberg he lived temperately with a German family whom his aunt, a German, knew.

Mentally and emotionally he developed prodigiously. In the last decade of the nineteenth century few spots in

Europe could have afforded a more complete contrast to Whitstable than Heidelberg. The air was charged with new ideas. The new drama of Ibsen and the new music of Wagner were loudly praised and loudly damned. *The Origin of Species* and Ernest Renan's *Life of Jesus,* in which Renan applied the method of the historian to the Biblical narrative, were avidly read and hotly debated.

Willie did not enroll in the University, but he attended some classes there. Kuno Fischer's lectures on philosophy aroused in him an interest that has remained all his life. In Heidelberg the boy took a few steps towards the agnosticism he was later to embrace. The seeds of skepticism had been sown in Whitstable when God failed to answer his prayer that his stammer be cured. The character of his uncle—lazy, selfish, dogmatic—did not increase his respect for religion. Now the heady conversations of Heidelberg stirred him up.

The Heidelberg year included cultural detours throughout Germany and into Switzerland. In Munich, Willie saw Ibsen drinking beer at the Maximilianerhof. He also began to write in earnest. He wrote a biography of Meyerbeer, despite the handicap of knowing nothing of music and never having heard any of Meyerbeer's operas. It was rejected and he burned the manuscript.

When he returned from Heidelberg the choice of a profession had to be settled. More sure of himself and more willing to take a stand, Willie refused to consider the church. After a six weeks' sortie into accountancy, which he loathed, he decided to become a physician, and

33

in the fall of 1892 entered the medical school attached to
St. Thomas' Hospital in London. He hadn't, he said later,
much interest in medicine at the time, but he was interested in living in London.

In London Willie lived in a boarding house at 11 Vincent Square, Westminster. His landlady was a cockney
woman named Mrs. Foreman, whose way with the English language so fascinated him that he dragged her into
Cakes and Ale, where she has no discernible connection
with anything else in the novel. Maugham occupied two
rooms on the ground floor, for which he paid a pound a
week and which he brightened up with a Moorish rug
and curtains of a bilious green. Years later, when he was
famous, he dropped by to drink a dish of tea with Mrs.
Foreman (just as Willie Ashenden in *Cakes and Ale*
dropped by to see Mrs. Hudson) and they talked of old
times. "Very artistic you was, wasn't you?" she said.

Although he did not, like Philip Carey, flunk a course
in medical school, Willie gave as little time to his medical studies as he dared and as much time as he could
manage to reading and writing. He read prodigiously.
While at St. Thomas' he made his way through English,
French, and Italian literature, and he also read some
philosophy and a lot of history and science.

His writing at this time was mostly one-act plays, fright-
fully realistic ones. Under the influence of Ibsen he probed
deep into the human soul, and thanks to his medical
training he could, he says, go into very elegant detail
about his character's venereal diseases and other shame-
ful ailments.

Despite his conviction that in this life our wills are the slaves of our emotions, Maugham has several times radically changed the course of his life by taking stock of a situation, consciously and deliberately making a decision, and thereafter following a new line of activity. At twenty-two he was more interested in writing plays than novels, but no manager would accept his plays. Maugham concluded that the managers might be more interested if he had two or three successful novels to his credit. At that time Fisher Unwin was publishing a series of short novels in what he called the Pseudonym Library, and Maugham first sent him two long short stories which he thought might add up to a volume. Unwin rejected these but wrote that he would be glad to consider a novel if Maugham had one on hand. Maugham thanked him kindly and, ten minutes later, began a novel.

As a part of his medical training Maugham in his fourth year worked as an obstetric clerk in the Lambeth slums near the hospital. His term of office lasted three weeks, and during this time he was on call day and night, and attended sixty-three confinements. This experience provided the material for his first novel, which he called *Liza of Lambeth*. He said he exercised little invention but simply put down what he saw and heard as plainly as possible. He would have liked to make his story more thrilling and picturesque, but the poverty of his imagination forced him to stick closely to the facts.

When he finished the novel Maugham sent it to Unwin, who three months later wrote him and invited him to call. Told that his novel had been accepted for publication, Maugham was too thrilled to drive a good bargain—a mistake he has never been guilty of since—and cheerfully signed the paper put before him. Almost immediately he began a second novel, *The Making of a Saint.* In a copy of it which I found in a secondhand bookstore Maugham wrote, "A novel written when the author was one & twenty, & he writes his name in it now with reluctance." Maugham has said that he wrote *Liza* when he was twenty-one, but the evidence points to twenty-two for both novels. It was not until 1896, when he was twenty-two, that he had the experiences on which he based *Liza.*

Liza of Lambeth was published in October, 1897. The edition was very small because there was much concern among the older members of the firm as to whether the novel should be published at all. On the day of its publication the office was in a state of nervous apprehension. So, presumably, was its author. Years later I was staying with him in Hollywood when he received his six author's copies of *The Hour Before the Dawn.* I asked him whether he was excited to see one of his books in print for the first time.

"Well," he said, "it's not like *Liza,* you know."

The small first edition of *Liza* provides an amusing bibliographical puzzle which throws some light on the difference in taste between the reading public of 1897 and 1958. In the novel as Maugham wrote it there appeared the word, "belly," a highly offensive word to most readers of the day. When he corrected the proof, Maugham told me, he deleted the shocking word. (Presumably no one objected to "dirty bitch" and "prostitute," for these epithets are hurled at the heroine in the first edition.) Nevertheless, it is still rumored that in a few copies of the first edition, "belly" is to be found. No bibliographer of Maugham claims to have seen one, and probably there is none. When the novel was reissued in 1930, "belly" was restored. There was no public outcry.

Liza of Lambeth was well reviewed, on the whole, and attracted considerable attention. Unwin had been astute enough to send copies to church dignitaries, and the author had the satisfaction of hearing that it had been damned by Basil Wilberforce in Westminster Abbey. The first edition sold out and a second was printed.

Written as it was before he learned his craft, *Liza* is worth examining for the evidence it provides of Maugham's native equipment as a writer. The novel is superior to four or five Maugham novels which follow it, and was repeatedly reissued between 1904 and 1930. Until *Of Human Bondage,* no Maugham novel achieved the same popularity, although one of them, *Mrs. Craddock,* is certainly superior to *Liza.*

The merit of the novel derives chiefly from Maugham's exact observation of people and places. There is no subtlety, and Maugham's attitude towards his slum characters is a bit condescending, but the characters, even the minor ones, are clearly defined and differentiated. The dialogue is pointed and apt, its realism heightened by the author's apology for toning down his heroine's salty language. The story moves at a rapid, sure pace and culminates in a grotesque scene of considerable power. What especially sets it off from most popular novels of the time is the complete absence of sentimentality and moralizing. Liza sins and she dies, but she does not repent first, nor is her death the wages of her sin.

While he was at St. Thomas', Maugham began the first of his notebooks, in which he set down dialogue for plays he hoped to write, scraps of conversation he had overheard, and generalizations about life. He kept a writer's notebook all his writing career, and by 1949 had filled fifteen large volumes. Although much of this material is personal and revealing, it was never set down as a record of his own mental and emotional life; it was intended only as raw material for his writing. Nor are the notebooks a journal; Maugham never tells us whose house he went to or whom he met. Even the earliest entries are remarkably objective and detached. There is almost no self-analysis or indication of how he felt about what he saw and recorded. Nevertheless, the entries for the years 1892–97 provide an insight into the kind of chap young Willie Maugham was, for when he published a selection of his notebooks, Maugham with characteristic honesty and candor included many of the callow observations and labored epigrams he had set down in his youth.

Experience has mellowed Maugham, but it has not much changed his convictions about the nature of man and God and the universe. Most of these convictions are implicit in what he wrote in his early notebooks. Everything in life is meaningless, he decided; pain and suffering are fruitless and futile. There is no object in life. At twenty-two he was a full-fledged skeptic. He did not believe in God because he saw no need to. God's existence can be neither proved nor disproved. The idea of an after-life is incredible. The spirituality of man is most apparent when he is eating a hearty dinner. One's philosophy is of little use in the ordinary affairs of life. Love of self is the mainspring of every man's actions; there would be very little altruism in the world if it were not a source of pleasure.

Because of his stammer, Maugham was never a mixer. He always stood aloof, viewing his fellow man with amused contempt and no excess of charity. He was early suspicious of what others call virtue and, like his fictional biographer Charles Strickland in *The Moon and Sixpence,* he has an unerring eye for the despicable motive in ac-tions having all the appearance of innocence. This is evi-dent in the early notebooks. People often feel the hungry, he observed, so that nothing may disturb their own enjoy-ment of a good meal. Seldom does a man love once and for all, and perhaps then only because his sexual instincts are not very strong.

If Maugham's clinical, disenchanted view of women was fostered by experience, the experience must have been early and bitter, for already at twenty-two he was snipping at them. Women exhibit less emotion at pain than men, he concedes, but that does not prove they bear it better, only that they feel it less. No man in his heart is quite so cynical as a well-bred woman.

Besides reading and writing, another activity—travel—varied the monotony of his medical training. In 1894, when he was twenty, Maugham made his first trip to Italy.

It was a cultural pilgrimage undertaken during the six weeks' Easter holiday, and he had twenty pounds to spend. From Pisa he hiked miles just to sit in the pine woods where Shelley had read Sophocles. In Florence he read Dante with the landlady's daughter, and admired everything Ruskin told him to admire. The following year he went again, and this time he discovered Capri, where he returned the next summer and where he wrote his second novel. With a friend from his Heidelberg days and an American colonel who had fought for the South in the Civil War, plus other assorted eccentrics, he argued about art and literature and tried to live down the shame of being a medical student, a coarse creature indifferent to beauty. In the fall he returned to St. Thomas'.

Maugham attended St. Thomas' for five years and earned his medical degree in 1897, when he was twenty-three. He is, therefore, Dr. Maugham and a member in good standing of the Royal College of Surgeons, but unlike Dr. A. J. Cronin, another physician-turned-popular-novelist, he does not insist that you use his title. In fact, I have never heard him or anyone else refer to it, and the only time I heard him give medical advice it was ignored. He told a man suffering from a hernia that he shouldn't ride horseback.

The success of *Liza*, published shortly before Maugham completed his medical studies, brought the writer to the attention of his superiors at St. Thomas' and got him an offer of a post there. However, elated by the success of his novel and against the advice of his publisher, Maugham decided to chuck medicine and devote himself to writing.

A year later, when he received his royalty check for *Liza,* he may have doubted the wisdom of his decision. Maugham's contract was a poor one, and despite the success of the novel, his take came to no more than a hundred dollars.

Many years later Maugham acknowledged that he had acted foolishly in abandoning medicine so precipitously. "It was idiotic. Absolutely idiotic. I could just as well have written at night and avoided the desperate financial struggle I had. I am sorry I abandoned medicine so soon for another reason. The chances of one's writing anything of permanent value before one is thirty are small. One wastes valuable themes trying to make a living."

Having abandoned medicine, Maugham entered upon his lean years, the beginning writer's classic period of struggle. "The first ten years I wrote, I never earned more than $500 a year," he said. "It was a constant struggle against poverty. My books were being published, but I hardly made enough on them to live."

Maugham struggled in picturesque surroundings, however. He settled in Seville, where he grew a mustache, smoked cigars, learned to play the guitar, and bought a broad-brimmed hat. He hankered for a flowing cape lined with green and red velvet, but couldn't afford it. Possibly that is why, eighteen years later, the dust cover of the first edition of *Of Human Bondage* shows Philip wearing this romantic garb.

He also wrote his third novel, which he called "The Artistic Temperament of Stephen Carey." Fortunately, as it turned out, no publisher would give him the money he wanted for it, for had this novel been published Maugham would have wasted the material from which he later wrought his masterpiece. Recently Maugham said of his unpublished autobiographical novel, "It finished with the hero at the age of twenty-four, which was my own age when I finished it; and it sent him to Rouen, which I knew only from two or three visits, instead of to Heidelberg, which I knew so well; and it made him study music, of which I knew nothing, instead of making him study painting, of which in later years I was to learn at least a little. . . . I never had the courage to read it again." Maugham gave the manuscript of this unpublished novel to the Library of Congress, on condition that it never be published.

Eight months after *Liza* appeared, Fisher Unwin brought out *The Making of a Saint.* Its subtitle—A Romance of Medieval Italy—suggests one reason for its failure. The novel was a product of Maugham's reading rather than his observation and experience. It was based on a story he had read in Machiavelli's *History of Florence.* As in *Liza,* the best thing about it is its dialogue which, although it has none of the realism of the first novel, is occasionally witty and anticipates the brilliant artificiality of the drawing-room comedies Maugham was to write in a few years. *The Making of a Saint* is also the first example of Maugham's use of the first person, later his favorite device for telling a story. Here, however, the narrator is a colorless person, unrelated to the worldly, detached teller of the later tales.

After a year in Spain Maugham went to Rome, where

he wrote his first full-length play, *A Man of Honour*. (*Schiffbruechig*, a one-act play written in German while he was living in Heidelberg, was produced in Berlin in 1902.) He planned to go to Greece to learn Greek, and to Cairo to learn Arabic. Instead, he returned to Seville, a heavenly city to live in, he said, in the flower of one's youth.

Before long, he was back in London, and with a friend of his own age took a small flat near Victoria Station. He wrote a number of short stories and sold them to now-forgotten magazines, and he continued to write novels and plays. The novels were published and respectfully reviewed, but they were never wildly popular. Maugham therefore was accepted by the intelligentsia and sought after by literary hostesses. He lunched out and dined out and weekended in country houses. "Augustus," an essay he wrote some fifty years later, describes life among the landed gentry at this time.

Maugham's most important work during this period, and his best novel before *Of Human Bondage*, was *Mrs. Craddock*, published in 1902. Although he wrote in my copy, "Oeuvre de jeunesse!" it is, in fact, a far more mature work than any he had so far produced, and anticipates his later novels in style and theme. In it, as in *Liza*, he used a setting he knew intimately and was to use again, the countryside of Kent near Whitstable. The novel recounts the birth and death of a high-born lady's passion for her low-born, physically attractive tenant farmer, whom she rashly marries. *Mrs. Craddock* is Maugham's first use of a theme that became a favorite—

the death of love. The death of love is not all tragedy; it has its compensations, for, all passion spent, Bertha Craddock belongs to herself again, and she exults in her hard-won emotional independence. Craddock obligingly dies after falling off his horse, Bertha finds she can enjoy reading again, and the novel ends on a note of optimism.

Mrs. Craddock is more autobiographical than it appears to be, for its two chief women characters, Bertha and Miss Ley, embody two sides of Maugham's character: the passionate, over-sensitive side that eventually loathes the person who has made inadequate response to his aggressive love-making; and the ironic, skeptical side, which sees the futility and absurdity of everyone, including himself. Miss Ley is also the first of a series of wise, tolerant, ironic, middle-aged women who infest Maugham's fiction.

We have it on Maugham's own authority that it isn't unusual for a novelist to put himself into two characters in one novel, or even to change his sex in the process. In his introduction to *Wuthering Heights*, written some forty-seven years after *Mrs. Craddock*, he says that Emily Brontë did just that.

In 1899, Fisher Unwin had brought out a volume called *Orientations*, which contains six of the short stories written about this time. Other stories written and published during these years are presumably lost, although one turned up and has an interesting subsequent history. In the summer of 1941, while doing research in the Library of Congress, I came across a Maugham short story, "The Happy Couple," which had appeared in *Cassell's Magazine* in 1908. Maugham was in Hollywood at the time, and I sent him a telegram in which I summarized the story and asked him whether he would like me to copy it and send it to him. He wrote back that he couldn't remember the story and was sure it was lousy. Why waste my time? Then it occurred to me that I could have the story photostated for a couple of dollars and perhaps Maugham would be amused to reread an early effort. I sent it to him and he thanked me, adding that he was surprised the story didn't date more than it did, and he might rewrite it. He rewrote it, using the same characters, plot, and title. The new "Happy Couple" appeared in the February, 1943, *Redbook*.

The theatre managers continued to reject his offerings, and Maugham in desperation sent *A Man of Honour* to the Stage Society, a highbrow organization which produced plays thought too good for the commercial theatre. On February 23 and 24, 1903, Maugham's tragedy was given two performances. Written five years before it was produced, *A Man of Honour* is pretty weak stuff, but although unrelievedly tragic, the play is transparently Maugham's. Its theme is the havoc wrought by a man who honorably marries a lower-class girl whom he has made pregnant.

Shortly after the two-night run of *A Man of Honour*, Maugham, feeling he was in a rut, went to live in Paris. He took a small, fifth-floor flat near the Lion de Belfort which afforded a fine view of the Montparnasse cemetery. Every evening he went to a cheap restaurant called the Chat Blanc where Arnold Bennett, also living in Paris at this time, occasionally dined. According to Bennett, the first time he saw him, Maugham, white with passion, was damning the French poet Heredia. The two men became friends of a sort and remained so until Bennett's death. A twofold bond held them together during these early years: both were struggling young writers and both stammered.

Despite their common affliction, there is evidence that Maugham was not extremely fond of Bennett, for years later he wrote, "Arnold was good company and I always enjoyed spending an evening with him, but I did not much like him. He was very cocksure and bumptious, and he was rather common. I do not say this of him depreciatingly, but as I might say of someone that he was short or fat." Also, "He was never what in England is technically known as a gentleman."

The tone and technique of this criticism are characteristic of Maugham. Taking as his subject a well-known person, he calls to our attention all sorts of weaknesses and vices, and then gently chides us for considering them of the slightest importance in our estimate of the man's worth. Edmund Burke, he wrote, was upright and abject, straightforward and shifty, disinterested and corrupt. But, he continues, let us not be censorious. Had Burke been born a gentleman with a fine estate and an ample income, no doubt he would have been as irreproachable as he is thought to be.

Possibly Maugham's vignette of Bennett was influenced by some reflections on his own gentility which appeared in Bennett's *Journal*, published shortly before Maugham wrote his piece. On March 3, 1905, when they were both living in Paris, Bennett made the following entry: "Somerset Maugham came up for tea. He has a very calm, almost lethargic demeanour. He took two cups of tea with pleasure and absolutely refused a third; one knew instantly from his tone that nothing would induce him to take a third. He ate biscuits and *gaufrettes* very quickly, almost greedily, one after the other, without a pause, and then suddenly stopped. He smoked two cigarettes furiously, in less time than I smoke one, and solidly declined a third. I like him."

The painter Gerald Kelly, a friend from these Paris days and the original of Lawson in *Of Human Bondage*, recounts another incident which was not likely to increase Willie's enthusiasm for his fellow author. "My recollection is that Maugham and Bennett heartily disliked each other at their first meeting, which I brought about. One evening Bennett had the nerve to correct Willie's French, which was usually extremely good. There was tension between them and I remember the general amusement at the look of rage in Willie's face."

Another occasional visitor to the Chat Blanc was Aleister Crowley, whom Maugham describes as a fake but not entirely a fake. He was a liar and boastful, but he had actually done some of the things he claimed to have done. He wrote verse, some of it good enough to be mistaken for bad Swinburne or Browning. Maugham says of him what he said of Bennett, that he enjoyed his company but didn't much like him. At any rate, he served Maugham well. He is the original of Oliver Haddo in *The Magician* and of Cronshaw in *Of Human Bondage*. Neither novel, of course, is a transcription of the facts. In the latter, Philip Carey took a bedraggled Cronshaw into his home and cared for him tenderly until his death. In actual fact, Maugham resolutely resisted an appeal telegraphed by Crowley: "Please send twenty-five pounds at once. Mother of God and I starving."

Maugham's life among the artists and writers of Paris from 1903 to 1905 supplied him with the material for Chapters 40–51 of *Of Human Bondage*, and contributed to his own profound knowledge of painting. However, before the end of 1905 he returned to London, still poor and unknown, a condition he was thoroughly fed up with. He had published several serious novels and had had a serious play produced, yet he wasn't making a decent living. He decided that he was not satisfied with the appreciation of a small band of intellectuals, and he had his doubts about their quality. He wanted the great public for his audience. Besides, he had found out that money is like a sixth sense without which you cannot make the most of the other five.

It was not long before he was making the most of all six. Here again Maugham changed the course of his life by analyzing a situation, reaching a decision, and embarking upon a new line of activity. He was determined to write a play that would be popular, and he decided that it should be a comedy. He had tried his hand at comedy a few years before when he wrote *Loaves and Fishes*, but the managers would have none of it because its hero was a worldly parson who intrigues to get a bishopric. (A few years later he turned the play into a novel published as *The Bishop's Apron*.) In order to find out what the public wanted, he studied the plays that were pulling in the crowds and concluded that his best chance was to write a comedy with a big part for an actress. Then, having made up his mind what sort of part would be likely to appeal to a leading lady, he wrote *Lady Frederick*. For once in his life Maugham had underrated the vanity of women. In one scene of the play Lady Frederick, in order to disillusion a youthful admirer, initiates him into the mysteries of her boudoir. She shows herself without makeup and with her hair in its natural state. No prominent actress of the day wanted to risk that. The managers continued to be indifferent.

Maugham then wrote *Mrs. Dot*, a pleasant little play which no one could possibly object to. The managers thought it too slight, and a popular actress suggested to Maugham that he liven things up by inserting a burglary scene. Maugham's next try was *Jack Straw*, a play with a big part for an actor, but he had no better success with this.

At last came the bit of luck that changed everything. Otho Stuart, manager of the Court Theatre in London, needed a play to fill in an odd six weeks while he was casting another play, and he took a chance on *Lady Frederick*. It opened on October 26, 1907, and was an immediate success, the objectionable scene becoming the hit of the show. *Lady Frederick* ran for eighteen months to solid houses. Within six months *Mrs. Dot, Jack Straw*, and another play, *The Explorer*, were produced. The first two were solid hits, the third not quite a failure. With four plays running simultaneously in London, Maugham was the talk of the town. *Punch* published a cartoon showing Shakespeare biting his nails before a poster advertising Maugham's plays. At thirty-three, Willie had finally hit the jackpot, which promptly began to clank out a stream of gold coins. It has been clanking them out ever since.

CHAPTER 3 ⚔

Years of Plenty (1908-1922)

Success changed the pattern of Maugham's life. No longer need he ride buses in his white tie and tails, nor feel embarrassed before footmen in country houses because his pajamas were shabby and his toilet articles modest. His income, which before had seldom exceeded $500 a year, shot up to that much a week, and he could play to the hilt his favorite role of wealthy young man about town. In 1907 and 1911 his portrait was painted by Gerald Kelly, the English painter he had known in Paris. In the second of these, called "The Jester," Willie is seated, and very elegant with top hat, mustache, and cane. Although his philosophy of life was deeply pessimistic at the time, he looks contented enough to purr.

Distinguished persons sought his acquaintance. The mass of the people had lost confidence in the aristocracy and landed gentry because of the muddle they had made of things during the Boer War, Maugham tells us, but the aristocracy and the landed gentry hadn't realized this and were as self-assured as ever. Maugham was entertained in homes where host and guests talked as if running the British Empire were their private business. When a general election was pending, they would discuss whether Tom should have the Home Office and whether Dick would be satisfied with Ireland.

All this was heady experience for a young man recently poor, but in his mind Maugham soon cut these gentry down to size. Few people have led so exciting and varied lives as Maugham, and even fewer have been so little dazzled by what has happened to them. However thrilling an experience, a vital part of Maugham remains unaffected and shrewdly observant. He said he did not find these people as brilliant as his fancy painted them. They were ill-informed about the ordinary affairs of life and seldom revealed any subtlety of intellect or liveliness of imagination. With his fondness for generalization, he concluded that running a country required a special talent unrelated to general intelligence or imagination.

Although his success was spectacular, Maugham took it as a matter of course. He had always assumed that he would one day be successful. Moreover, he lacks the quality of being surprised at anything. One day shortly after his rise to fame, Maugham was dining at his club and overheard a conversation about himself. A fellow member whom he didn't know was telling a guest that he knew Maugham well and that his head was now so swollen that he couldn't get a hat big enough to fit him. According to Maugham, this wasn't so. He was amused by what he is careful to call his notoriety, but he was not impressed by it. A *Notebook* entry for 1908, more personal than most, states that the net value of his success was that it freed him from financial uncertainties. He hated having to scrape and save to make ends meet. Still, Maugham's passion for money was not primarily because money enabled him to indulge his epicurean tastes. He wanted money because he thought it would give him independence. It enabled him to tell the whole world to go to hell, and figuratively—occasionally literally—he has been doing so ever since.

With his new wealth Maugham was able to indulge his bent for travel, and in 1908 he visited Greece. In Athens he had an experience which seems to have shocked him at the time but later would have amused his sardonic sense. He was in the theatre of Dionysus, and from where he was sitting he could see the blue Aegean. He thought of the great plays that had been acted on that stage before him, and cold shivers ran down his spine. A group of Greek students came by and one of them asked Maugham if he would like to hear him recite something from the stage. Assuming that the young Greek would recite a noble passage of Sophocles or Euripides, Willie urged him to do so. The boy clambered onto the stage, struck an attitude, and spouted forth a bombastic speech from *Cyrano de Bergerac.*

Success was very satisfying, but one by-product of it was unpleasant. Despite his frequent protests to the contrary, Maugham has never fully recovered from the mortifying effects of it. So long as he wrote highbrow plays and unsuccessful novels, Maugham was looked upon as a promising young writer and an intellectual in good standing, and he took a modest pride in this honorable condition. But when he had the audacity to produce four popular plays simultaneously, he was ignominiously dropped by the intellectuals of the day, and their descendants have never picked him up. With few exceptions, today's intellectuals read and enjoy his work but speak condescendingly of it, as they might of a comic strip they follow.

This has long exasperated Maugham, who would like critical as well as popular acclaim and feels he is entitled to somewhat more of the former than he has received. He would never, however, voice such a view. It is his way to claim for his work no more merit than the meanest critic will allow it to have. He is, he says, but a teller of tales, a spinner of yarns, a writer of exciting but meaningless adventure. This, of course, is sheer nonsense. Every story he has written is permeated with his own view of life, and it is this view—whether it is profound or superficial, cynical or realistic—that gives his stories their special quality.

When the intellectuals took to despising him, Maugham realized that he didn't care for intellectuals. His stories frequently ridicule their pretensions, and the opening chapters of *Christmas Holiday* satirize them magnificently. Scorning the intelligentsia which scorned him, this elegant, fastidious, upper-class Britisher began to champion the lower classes, as he calls them. They should and they will inherit the earth, though he hopes they will wait to do so until he is dead.

The irony of this situation is that Maugham is, above

all, an intellectual—far more of an intellectual than most writers and with a better claim to the title than have most of the intellectuals who speak slightingly of his work. *A Writer's Notebook* shows how early and earnestly he sought to discover a meaning in life. He has always read with pleasure the kind of books which most people consider heavy going. Few professors of literature know English, American, or French literature as he knows them. Maugham's mind has a breadth seldom encountered among even the best-educated persons. Unlike most intellectuals, he wears his learning lightly; you could spend days with him without realizing that he had any more education than, say, the average Oxford graduate.

Although some of the critics, as well as the intelligentsia, looked down on his spectacular success, Maugham decided to continue being successful. Now that he had learned the formula, he cranked out one frothy comedy after another. *Penelope,* in which Marie Tempest was starred, was good enough to be successfully revived years later. Maugham also gained his first American public; his plays were produced in New York and were almost as well received there as in London.

Maugham now felt rich enough to have a home of his own, and in 1911 he bought a Georgian house at 6 Chesterfield Street in Mayfair. Here for the first time he played a role in which he was to become famous, that of host to the international set. At one of his dinners Billie Burke was the guest of honor. She had played Mrs. Dot in the American production of this play, and her acting was so remarkable that Maugham attributed the success of the play largely to her. He showed her around the house and Miss Burke admired everything extravagantly.

"You ought to like it," Maugham told her. "You paid for it."

The drawing room of 6 Chesterfield Street contained a portrait of Billie Burke, so that with slight variation Maugham was able to repeat his gallant witticism whenever he had guests.

Maugham says that between 1898 and 1933 he wrote thirty plays. Actually, we have the titles and text of thirty-two that he wrote, revised, translated, or adapted, and his word for several curtain raisers that were lost because they were not returned by the managers and there were no other copies. The discrepancy between these figures is explained by the fact that Maugham would like us to forget some of his plays. The collected edition includes only eighteen of the thirty-two. (The public's reception of a play had little to do with its inclusion in the collected edition. *The Letter*, one of the three most popular Maugham plays in England, was excluded, and three flops made the grade.)

A study of the record reveals some surprising statistics. One Maugham play was written and performed in German; three were translations, (two from French, one from Italian—all flops); one, an adaptation from Molière, was designed and performed (eight times) as the first part of Strauss' opera *Ariadne in Naxos;* six have never been published; only about half are named in Maugham's extensive autobiographical writing.

The number of performances in New York and London

varied greatly. Maugham's brand of sophisticated drama was much more popular in his own country than here. Only one play, *The Constant Wife*, starring Ethel Barrymore, ran longer in this country than in England. *Our Betters*, which satirizes Americans, ran five times as long in London as in New York; *Penelope* ran five times as long on home ground; *The Sacred Flame*, ten times; *Home and Beauty* (*Too Many Husbands* in New York), fifteen times. One play (*"The Road Uphill"*) was never produced anywhere; one (*The Mask and the Face*) was produced in this country but not in England; eight were put on in England but not here. *The Circle*, often called Maugham's best play, had only an average run in both countries. *For Services Rendered*, which I consider his finest play, was a mild flop in London and a resounding one in New York.

Just before this play was produced in 1932, Maugham announced that, several years before, he had decided to give up playwriting as soon as he had written four plays he had long had in mind. Anyone who thinks Maugham's plays are airy trifles should examine these. One is a melodrama, one a tragedy, and two are sardonic comedies which made their audiences squirm more than laugh. Each play is a vehicle for saying something Maugham wanted very much to say.

The first of the four was *The Sacred Flame*, and it probably deserves most of the brickbats heaved its way. But the other three are among Maugham's best. *The Breadwinner* ridicules charmingly selfish adolescents and their frivolous, empty-headed mothers. Each generation considered the play a ringing indictment of the other generation and a libel on itself. *For Services Rendered* failed for equally obvious reasons. It is a bitter anti-war play, not at all what audiences expected from Maugham, and they resented the assault on their emotions when they had come to be amused. Had an unknown dramatist written it, it would probably have been hailed as a masterpiece.

Sheppey, the last play, was produced in London in 1933, but not until 1944 in New York. Although tense and dramatic in spots, it changes course in midstream: the first act, a play in itself, is high comedy; the other two are painfully serious. Maugham said he expected it to flop, and it did.

Maugham is a cautious man, and he didn't write flops until he could well afford them. In fact, he wrote so many successful plays that they began to bore him, and in 1911 he decided to take time out and write a novel that was begging to be written. Had he not done so, the chances are that he would be very little read today, for the novel he set himself to write was *Of Human Bondage.*

Of Human Bondage is about three times as long as any other Maugham novel. It took him two years to write. Before he finished it, World War I had started, and he corrected the proofs by candlelight in a little village in Flanders in 1914. The novel appeared the following year, the American edition antedating the English by one day. The editions were small—the English edition was 5000 copies—because no Maugham novel had been extremely popular up to that time. Consequently, the first edition is now a valuable collector's item.

Of Human Bondage was not immediately popular, for during the war few readers could give their undivided attention to the ordeal of Philip Carey. Every year, however, its reputation increased, helped not a little in this country by Dreiser's ecstatic review. Today it is generally recognized as Maugham's masterpiece.

Maugham, who believes that a masterpiece is likely to come, if at all, as the culminating point of a laborious career, does not share this view. He is not flattered by the notion that in the succeeding forty-five years he never again produced anything as good. He always seems a little bored when you mention the novel, and when he is forced to refer to it, belittles it. He does not think it will live. Posterity, he says, is not inclined to occupy itself with books as long as *Of Human Bondage*. He thinks one or two of his comedies have a better chance for survival, and one or two of his short stories many continue to be read because they depict a way of life that has passed. He thinks that some of the writing in *Of Human Bondage* is sloppy and the grammar faulty. (He was, however, shocked when I pointed out that in one sentence in Chapter 52 he had said the opposite of what he meant.) He did not plan to write a great novel. His motive for writing the book was strictly therapeutic. "I wrote that book to free myself of an intolerable obsession, to rid myself of ghosts. From that point of view it was successful. After I corrected the proofs, I found that all the ghosts were laid. They never troubled me, or crossed my mind again."

Maugham, of course, exaggerates the defects of the

novel and ignores its merits. One has only to compare it
with the novel that preceded it—*The Magician*—to realize to what extent Maugham had mastered his craft in
a half-dozen years. *Of Human Bondage* is the only
Maugham novel in which the reader feels a deep com-
passion for the sufferings of humanity. It is the only one
in which Maugham reached for the stars. In the other
novels Maugham aimed lower and, in the best of them,
came closer to his mark. His skill fashioned a brilliant
novel out of a minimum of setting, plot, character, and
theme. Everything is pared down to essentials; Dr.
Maugham scalpeled away all the fat—and some of the
nerve and sinew. The late novels have the sparkle, the
clarity and perfection of a well-cut diamond—and some
of its hardness. There is something bloodless in their technical perfection. You enjoy them enormously, but you are
not much moved by them. *Of Human Bondage* is less perfect, but its raw material was Willie Maugham's own
thoughts, feelings, and experiences. He pondered their significance for years and then, recollecting in the tranquility
of middle age the violent emotions of his youth, he wrote
this rich, vital, abundant novel.

Consider its many settings: vicarage life in Blackstable,
school life in Tercanbury, intellectual life in Heidelberg
at the end of the century, bohemian life in Paris, and
London sixty years ago. Each of these is drawn in detail,
and each in itself has the scope of a novel. Or look at its
cast of characters. Alroy Kear of *Cakes and Ale,* Julia
Gosselyn of *Theatre,* and Larry Darrell of *The Razor's
Edge* are brilliant characterizations, but they are pallid

creatures beside the men and women who crowd the pages of *Of Human Bondage*—Uncle William and Aunt Louisa Carey, Fanny Price, Miss Wilkinson, Hayward, Athelny, Norah, Sally, and especially Mildred, the slut who rides herd on Philip's life. Even the minor characters are unforgettable—Ruth Chalice, Clutton, Cronshaw, Griffiths, and Leonard Upjohn, the first of a series of unflattering portraits of the critic.

The impact of these people and places on the shy, introverted Philip Carey provides the story, and it is such a good story that it has held thousands of readers who have never given a thought to what Maugham has to say in the novel. There is a clue to this in the title. Man is in bondage to his emotions, which rule his life. It is an illusion that experience and rational thought can affect one's actions. Young people as they grow up suffer unbearably because, unless they are fools, they must gradually realize that all they have been taught about life is a lie. Yet they in turn contribute to another's disillusionment through a power within them that is stronger than themselves. In all human relationships—friendship, love, or what have you—Philip finds the facts to be different from the spurious ideals on which he had been nurtured. Most bitter of all is the realization that one is not the captain of one's fate. A man can despise a woman as he despises Mildred, seeing her exactly as she is, without charity and without idealization; yet, unable to break his bondage to her, he can passionately desire her and suffer any humiliation rather than lose her.

As the rejected title, "Beauty from Ashes," suggests, the

tone of the novel is somber but not hopelessly pessimistic. A man can attain a measure of contentment if he learns and accepts certain unalterable facts of life. (It is evidence of Maugham's power as a storyteller that the majority of readers enjoy the novel while rejecting its philosophy.) To be happy, one must first accept the fact that in this world everyone is for himself. Man does what he thinks is good for him, and if it happens to be good for others as well, he is called unselfish, but he is not. One's life is like the pattern of an oriental rug, simple or elaborate, subtle or obvious, but in every case meaningless. There is no God and there is nothing after this life.

Besides the fact that it was written early in his career, another reason Maugham does not consider *Of Human Bondage* his best novel is that it is his least characteristic work. It is Dickensian in its rich detail; the later novels are as spare as a Robert Frost lyric. In it Maugham unburdened his heart and mind like a penitent in the confessional. Philip Carey is confused, egotistical, masochistic, intolerant. He lives life naively and passionately. The narrator of the later novels is as remote and God-like as a cloistered monk, if more worldly and less reverent. He acknowledges that he has weaknesses like the rest of us, but he never reveals them. He is detached, a trifle cynical, and, above all, reticent. From his point of view, Philip Carey's naked revelation of his inmost nature shows a deplorable lack of taste.

Maugham has always been able to stand aside and look at his own life as if it were someone else's. He also has more than the average man's ability to plan his life and follow out the plan. Because he has a tidy mind, he wanted to make a pattern of his life. The pattern he planned was rich and varied, and it included marriage. In 1915, a year chiefly important in Maugham's life for the publication of *Of Human Bondage*, he married a divorcée named Syrie Wellcome, a woman as unlike Sally Athelny (whom Philip plans to marry at the end of the novel) as it would be possible to find. Mrs. Maugham was the daughter of Dr. Thomas Barnardo, an Irish philanthropist who founded a group of children's homes. She was a small woman with a small head, red cheeks, great vitality, and plenty of determination. The Maughams had one child, a daughter named Elizabeth, called Liza after the heroine of her father's first novel. When the Maughams were divorced in 1927, the injured party is said to have been consoled by a cash settlement of a million dollars. Syrie Maugham became a decorator. She died in 1955.

After her parents were divorced, Liza lived with her mother and met her father only once a year, when he took her to lunch at Claridge's. These were not relaxed affairs. Father and daughter hardly knew each other until after Liza's marriage to Vincent Paravicini, when she and her husband visited Maugham frequently. The Paravicinis presented Maugham with two grandchildren, and Maugham seems to have been a somewhat more dutiful grandfather than father, although more conscientious than doting. Liza and her children lived in the United States during the Second World War, and were necessarily subjected to all sorts of vicious American influences, and Maugham worried lest the children acquire a taste for coke and American slang.

In the manner of most divorced husbands, Maugham made few references to his ex-wife, but I recall one. We were partners at bridge, and one of our opponents, acidly commenting on the fact that Maugham was holding all the good cards, remarked that he must be exceedingly unlucky in love. Maugham pretended that he didn't understand the allusion, and our opponent explained that he had in mind the old adage, lucky at cards, unlucky in love. Maugham said, "Oh. I thought you meant my wife was unfaithful to me."

Fatherhood did not blind Maugham to what he considered the defects of his daughter's character, any more than friendship obscured the faults of his friends. I remember his concern that Liza seemed to have no notion of the value of money. She had always had plenty of it, and she assumed she always would. Once someone asked, what would you do if you had a dozen people coming to dinner and the cook suddenly left.

"That's easy," said Liza. "I'd take them all out to dinner."

Maugham shook his head.

Once, when Liza and I were both visiting her father in Beverly Hills, she playfully suggested that he put her in a story, and her indulgent parent replied mildly, "I don't think you would like it very much if I did." When the Paravicini marriage was breaking up after World War II, Maugham wrote me as objective an analysis of it as you would expect him to make of the marriage of two of his characters.

The immediate effect of Maugham's own marriage seems to have been to stimulate his interest in travel. In fact, so varied and extensive was his itinerary during these years that it is difficult to see how he managed a proper honeymoon, not to speak of fatherhood. However, not all his travels were for pleasure. When war broke out in 1914, Maugham joined a Red Cross ambulance unit as a medical officer and spent about a year in France and Belgium. The notebook entries for this period show that he observed men under the stress of war as shrewdly and objectively as he had observed social life in Mayfair. Nor was he unhappy because he was no longer leading a life of ease. Maugham has always welcomed change and new experience, and until he was old he never liked to linger in one spot longer than three months. Despite the hard work, the cold, the inadequate bathing facilities, the bad food (he never mentions the danger), he enjoyed himself very much. It was delightful to have no responsibilities. He could understand why some men have the time of their lives during the war.

In 1915 he left the Red Cross and went to Italy, paying another visit to Capri, his favorite island. In Rome he wrote *Our Betters,* one of his most brilliant drawing-room comedies and surely one of his half-dozen best plays. It was first produced in New York in 1917 and caused a sensation, for most of its women characters are rich Americans who married titles and lead scandalous lives in England. Nevertheless, *Our Betters* is not, strictly speaking, satire. Maugham does not scorn or ridicule his morally worthless characters, nor does he moralize. Moralizing he has always considered as ill-bred as praying in public. Maugham gets too much satisfaction from observing the follies and vices of his fellow beings not to look upon them charitably. In this play, as in most of his plays, he has something to say: People who shun their responsibilities and lead pleasure-loving, worthless lives become worthless people. He says the same thing in *The Circle*. You can easily miss the lesson, however, for he does not underline it, and your attention is held by the witty dialogue, the casual, amoral misbehavior of the characters, and the rapid succession of dramatic situations.

The trip to Italy was only a respite between war jobs, for Maugham soon went to Geneva, where under cover of writing he worked as a spy for the Intelligence Department. Maugham says he found spying routine, unexciting, and ridiculous. This may explain why the stories based on his spying experience (a collection called *Ashenden*, which Maugham inexplicably calls a novel, although he reprinted them in his collected short stories) are not among Maugham's best. It is an amusing thesis that a spy's job is as safe and monotonous as a floorwalker's, but the stories which develop it are not likely to provide exciting reading. Only "Giulia Lazzari" is actually a spy story, and it is a good one. The others contain brilliant characterizations and little, if any, plot.

Whatever their limitations as fiction, the *Ashenden*

stories were accepted as fact by Goebbels, who, speaking over the radio during World War II, cited them as examples of British cynicism and brutality. The British themselves seem to have been deceived by their verisimilitude: the book was required reading for persons entering the Intelligence Department. As fiction the *Ashenden* stories lack the qualities which mark Maugham's best short stories—exotic setting and a good plot. Maugham's imagination here seems to have been hampered by too much fact.

During the war Maugham successfully played the role of an expatriate author residing in a neutral country. Despite his spying chores, he continued to write. In the fall of 1915 he wrote *Caroline,* later called *The Unattainable,* a surprisingly feeble successor to the scintillating *Our Betters.* It is a three-act comedy which, its author later admitted, might better have ended with the first act. Maugham sent the manuscript to London, where it was immediately put into production, and he went over for the final rehearsals. It opened on February 8, 1916, and thanks to its star, Irene Vanbrugh, had a considerable run.

Shortly after the opening, Maugham sailed for New York, ostensibly to arrange for the American production of *Caroline.* But he was still a secret agent and his real purpose was to prepare himself for a trip to Russia, where he was instructed to do his bit to keep Russia in the war and prevent the Bolsheviks from seizing power. Three months after his arrival in Petrograd, the Kerensky government was set up and Maugham's plans came to naught.

He observed Kerensky in action and was not impressed. Afterwards, Maugham nursed the delusion that had he gone to Russia earlier, he might have succeeded and thus changed the course of history.

Almost a year elapsed between Maugham's arrival in this country and his arrival in Russia, and if he later regretted the delay, his readers have no reason to, for during that time he made his first trip to the South Seas and gathered the material for some of his finest stories. He was to travel to Russia via Japan, and because he was ailing he got permission to detour for six months to the South Pacific. On the way he visited the Hawaiian Islands. In Honolulu he inspected the Chinese quarter and the Red Light district.

He visited a number of islands of the Samoan group, and then Fiji, Tonga, and Tahiti. Tahiti he was especially interested in because Paul Gauguin had lived there and he had long contemplated a novel based on the painter's life. Following his usual practice, Maugham made extensive notes of people and places in and around Papeete, and these so accurately and unflatteringly reflect their originals that after the novel was published Maugham was never again very welcome in Tahiti.

The novel, of course, was *The Moon and Sixpence.* In character and setting it is very different from *Of Human Bondage,* but it develops a similar and favorite Maugham theme: man's powerlessness to control his emotions and order his own destiny. In the novel Blanche Stroeve, a placid, meek woman gripped by a passion for a man she despises, deserts the husband who had rescued her from the gutter for a lover who proclaims his indifference to her and callously shatters her life and Dirk Stroeve's. But it is the painter Strickland's passion, not sexual but creative, that is the center of the novel. Maugham has often been damned as no more than a competent literary hack. He is too well-bred to refute such a canard openly. There is a kind of answer to the charge, however, in his many portraits of the artist and in his several analyses of the creative instinct, that mysterious life force which drives the artist, indifferent to monetary reward and the judgment of his peers, to fashion beauty out of the chaos of the world in the torment of his soul. Maugham implies that he too has known such divine and unprofitable ecstasy.

One would be hard put to find two persons more superficially unlike than the disciplined, articulate, gentlemanly Mr. Maugham and the ruthless, demoniac Charles Strickland of the novel, yet they are not so unlike as they seem. Although he prizes his breeding above his talent and lives decorously, Maugham has always been fascinated by rogues, geniuses, and other eccentrics who flout the laws of society. He is never sure that their way of life is not more satisfying than his. Strickland's fierce determination to be absolutely free, the merciless way he mows down all those who stand in his way, his complete indifference to the opinions of others are Maugham as he would like to be. He deplores his own despicable weakness of considering others. He yearns to be as ruthless as Strickland, and sometimes he steels himself to it.

Two minor characters in the novel are early examples

of familiar Maugham fictional types. One is Captain Nichols, a rogue who so intrigued his creator that he retained him, name and all, and gave him a bigger part in a later novel. The other is Mrs. Strickland, the first of a series of vampires whom Maugham excoriates for their charming gift of sympathy and their faculty for battening on the genius of others.

Maugham has many faithful female readers, but they deplore what they call his unfair attitude toward their sex. *The Moon and Sixpence,* the first novel written after his marriage, crackles with acid observations about women, especially regarding their absurd over-emphasis on love. You gather there is little to be hoped for from the sex unless, like Ata in this novel, they are kept ignorant, barefoot, and out of men's way.

The Tahitian visit was not the only one on this trip which had direct literary consequences. There was also an extended, though involuntary, stay at Pago Pago. The ship was scheduled to remain in port for only twenty-four hours, and Maugham went ashore to spend the night at the town's primitive hotel. When he and the other passengers tried to return to the ship, they learned that an epidemic of chicken pox had broken out and they were required to remain ashore for a period of quarantine. Among the other passengers were a missionary, his wife, and an ex-prostitute who had boarded the ship at Honolulu after the Hawaiian authorities had frowned upon her means of livelihood. In his notes Maugham describes her as follows: "Plump, pretty in a coarse fashion, perhaps not more than twenty-seven: she wore a white dress and a large white hat, and long white boots from which her calves, in white cotton stockings, bulged."

Maugham used these very words to describe the girl in the story he wrote about her and the missionary, whom he called Davidson. The character of Sadie Thompson owes nothing to the original except physical resemblance, for Maugham never spoke to her. The fact is that nothing much happened during that enforced stay in Pago Pago, but it did rain incessantly. While he was there Maugham planned his short story and made a rough draft of it, but he did not complete it until 1920. Called "Miss Thompson," it was published in Mencken and Nathan's *Smart Set*, after practically every other magazine editor in New York had rejected it.

Ironically, Maugham's popular reputation rests largely on his connection with a play he didn't write—*Rain*. Maugham wrote only the short story, and John Colton and Clemence Randolph are the authors of the play. In Maugham's opinion there wasn't a play there.

The drama *Rain* came into being in a curious way. In 1921 Maugham and Colton occupied rooms across the hall from each other in the Hollywood Hotel in Hollywood. One night, unable to sleep, Colton knocked on Maugham's door and asked if he had anything to read. Maugham lent him the proof sheets he had just received of a book called *The Trembling of a Leaf*, which contained "Miss Thompson." The next morning the two writers met in the dining room and Colton looked bleary-eyed. "I read that story of yours, the one you call 'Miss Thompson,' and I stayed awake all night thinking of what a good play it would make. I'd like to try my hand at turning it into one." "Go ahead," Maugham said. "It's all yours." The men shook hands on the deal.

When the book was published, other dramatists got the same idea, and one of them offered Maugham's agent $7000 for the rights to it. Colton was extremely disturbed when he heard about this. He didn't have $7000 and he didn't even have a contract. He had only that handshake. Maugham was on the other side of the world when his agent, who knew something of the deal with Colton, got in touch with him. A few days later she received a cable from Maugham: "The handshake still stands."

Maugham had no reason to regret his gesture. *Rain* became one of the great successes of the theatre, although both the English and American productions were slow to get off the ground. The American production came first, opening in New York on November 7, 1922. The out-of-town reviews had been unfavorable and New York was at first cool. But soon Jeanne Eagels soared to stardom in the play, and it ran more than twice as long as any Maugham-written play has run in this country.

The English production, which did not appear until May, 1925, got under way with even more difficulty. Tallulah Bankhead, then living in London, had been chosen to play Sadie, and she gives us her version of the facts in a chapter of her autobiography called "Ambushed by Somerset Maugham." Tallulah believed herself a natural for the part and was thrilled to be offered it. She traveled all the way to New York to see Jeanne Eagels' Sadie, and when she learned that the show was playing in Pittsburgh, she pursued her quarry there. On the ship going back to England, she played Sadie Thompson's records in her cabin and practiced the part. At the first rehearsal she considered herself one hundred per cent Sadie.

But Willie Maugham didn't. After the first rehearsal he avoided Tallulah, and after the second she was fired and Olga Lindo got the part. Maugham sent Tallulah a consolation prize of a hundred pounds and the suggestion that she dissipate her grief abroad. Tallulah, according to Tallulah, spat it back to him in a letter that took her four days to compose. She quotes a friend who quotes Maugham as having said that the greatest mistake of his professional career was not letting Tallulah Bankhead play Sadie Thompson. It may be so, but it does not sound like Maugham.

Rain opened in London and was, says Tallulah, an immediate flop. This seems to be a slight rearrangement of the facts. The English *Rain* ran 150 performances, 500 fewer than the American production, it is true, but a run longer than most of the English productions of Maugham's plays.

This, of course, is not the whole history of *Rain*, or even of Tallulah's connection with it. She revived the play in New York in 1935 (most of the critics backed up Maugham's judgment). By that time sixty Sadies had played it in stock, Sally Rand had played it in barns up and down the eastern coast, and Lenore Ulric had played it in Flatbush. Gloria Swanson, Joan Crawford, and Rita Hayworth made movies of it, and June Havoc was Sadie in a musical version. Colton, Randolph, and Maugham split royalties of over a million dollars.

But Maugham never changed his opinion that the whole thing was a mistake. The first time he saw the play he went with Colton. When it was over, Colton turned to him and anxiously asked him what he thought of it. Maugham answered, "I think 'Miss Thompson' is a good short story."

CHAPTER 4

Maugham and "I"

I FIRST met Somerset Maugham in the fall of 1923, at the old Shoreham Hotel in Washington. One of the passions of Maugham's life is bridge, and since I had some local reputation as a bridge player in those days, I was invited by a mutual friend to make up a foursome. I had recently read *Of Human Bondage* and was in a dither over the prospect of meeting its author.

Although I remember a number of remarks Maugham made that evening, I have only a general impression of what he looked like. He was only forty-nine at the time, yet his face already had the bitter, disillusioned look which his readers think appropriate. He was shorter than I expected, he wore a monocle, and his voice struck me as very, very British. (As a matter of fact, it isn't. Maugham has lived too little in England to speak pure Oxford English or any other English dialect in its pure form, but he speaks a reasonably good facsimile thereof.)

"G-g-good evening. Will you put your coat there?"

I was introduced to Gerald Haxton, his secretary, an American who seemed even more British than Maugham.

His manner was more relaxed and breezy than Maugham's, and he immediately put me at my ease. The bridge table was already set up. We cut for deal and partners and began to play. Maugham was my partner for the first rubber.

I suspect that I played very badly, for in addition to being nervous I was at that moment much more interested in Maugham than in bridge. I know now that Maugham was bored by my persistent questioning, but only occasionally did he indicate it. He gave courteous attention to everything I said, he answered my questions, but he rarely volunteered a remark. He is always embarrassed by any reference to his own writing, but I didn't realize it at the time. I was intrigued by the titles of several of his novels and asked him what he thought constituted a good title.

"A good title," said Maugham, "is the title of a book that's successful."

"That isn't much help to a writer when he has to choose a title."

"No, it isn't."

"I think *The Moon and Sixpence* is a very good title."

"Do you? Do you know what it means? People tell me it's a good title but they don't know what it means."

"What does it mean, Mr. Maugham?"

"It means reaching for the moon and missing the sixpence at one's feet."

"Oh, I see. Strickland."

"Yes."

"There's a title of a new novel that I think is an awfully good title," I said.

"What is it?"

"I can't quite remember."

"I hardly think it's a good title if you can't remember it. Did you bid?"

I also tried to discover what he thought of some of the masterpieces of English and American literature. Most of those I mentioned he didn't rate very highly, but he had a few kind words for some. He praised George Eliot's skill in weaving together the separate strands of *Middlemarch*. He liked Benjamin Franklin. He thought *David Copperfield* a very great novel, though full of obvious faults. His praise of a novel was usually balanced by reservations. He was kinder to poets than to novelists.

His judgments were incisive, and, as I later discovered, he was never unhappy when they differed from those of professional critics. He thought *The Scarlet Letter* overrated; he said it was built on a false premise. A woman of Hester's spirit would not have stayed around to incur the wrath of her fellow townsmen; she would simply have gone elsewhere to have her baby. In order to write the novel he wanted to write, Hawthorne had been guilty of making Hester behave out of character. He seemed to regard this sin of Hawthorne's as far more heinous than Hester's.

Gertrude Atherton's sensational novel, *Black Oxen*, had recently been published, and Maugham told me an amusing anecdote about her. He said she was convinced that the breath of a cow had remarkable life-giving qualities, and in order to profit by them she had had a pipe installed from the cow's quarters to hers. While she slept, the perfume of the cow's breath was wafted into her bedroom, and she arose the next morning a finer, calmer, more healthy woman.

Maugham always relished the absurd and unexpected in human behavior. He was touched by the self-sacrifice of a prostitute who sent her daughter to a convent school, and delighted when he heard of a college president who appointed his ex-mistresses to teaching positions in his college.

What I recall most clearly about that evening was a curious little incident that occurred toward the end. It disconcerted me at the time, and only later did I realize how characteristic of Maugham it was. When the game was over and we had put on our coats, Maugham and Haxton escorted us to the door. The elevator was just opposite and I rang for it. I thanked my host and said goodnight. The elevator was slow in coming and we continued to stand there. It did not appear for three or four minutes and they seemed like fifteen, for although the others of us chatted lightly and foolishly, as people do when they have nothing to say and must pass the time, Maugham said not one word. He has always endeavored to keep social chatter at a minimum by not engaging in it himself, and now he held his peace. He had said a courteous goodnight. Why say anything more?

At the time of our first meeting I knew nothing of Maugham's life. He didn't bother to mention that he was just back from Rangoon and Mandalay and en route to Mexico and the Caribbean islands. Years later I learned

that after the fiasco of his Russian expedition he spent
two years in a sanatorium in the north of Scotland recov-
ering from an attack of tuberculosis.

Most people would look back on such an experience
with horror; Maugham professes to have loved it. He says
that during the day he studied his fellow patients and
added to his knowledge of human nature. He had long
rejected the sentimental notion that pain and suffering
ennoble. Illness, he observed, twists the character.

At six o'clock he had his dinner in bed, and then he
was alone. He reveled in the silence and privacy of his
room, its immense windows wide open to the starry night.
His imagination, he said later, was never more nimble.
His spirits were high. Clutching a pencil in his mittened
hand, he dashed off one of his most rollicking comedies,
Home and Beauty. (He has never seen it performed; he
was still in the sanatorium when it was produced in this
country and in England.) He also wrote *The Moon and
Sixpence*.

I suspect that Maugham looks back on those years with
satisfaction because he knows that during that time he
came of age as a writer. Despite the fact that his greatest
novel and one of his best plays are pre-sanatorium, the
work that follows shows a maturity and control which is
not present in the earlier work.

Healthy once more and footloose, Maugham took to the
open road again. He is a traveler of an extinct breed not
likely to regenerate in these days of high taxes and Iron
Curtains. One of the advantages of authorship, he says, is
that you can practice your profession wherever you are.

For many years Maugham roamed over the world. He has visited almost every country on every continent, and often he has found himself going around the world because it was the shortest way home. He himself can no longer recall each journey, but his notebooks provide data for the curious. The trip to the South Seas in 1916–17 was his first extended journey. In 1920, after he had recovered from tuberculosis, he went to China; in 1921 to the Federated Malay States, Indo-China, and back to China. The following year he visited Australia and a number of islands of the Malay Archipelago and spent three months in Java. In 1923 he took in Central and South America; in 1924 he went back to the Malay States and to Borneo and Siam. He says he made no more trips until 1937, when he went to India for the winter; but the record shows that he returned to Borneo in 1929. He does not count minor excursions to places like Chicago, Hollywood, Nicosia, Seville, and Texas. The sixty-six letters, postal cards, telegrams, and cablegrams from him which I have preserved come from thirteen different places in six countries on four continents, and most of them date from a period later than his extensive traveling.

Maugham travels for the same reason most of us travel —because he likes to—and he has traveled widely and often because he had ample means and leisure. He is a man with a fearful sense of responsibility—except, perhaps, to his family—and a strong will, and at home he cannot often bring himself to shirk what his conscience tells him he should do. But traveling gave him a sense of freedom. Time seemed to stretch out before him and he could fritter away the hours without feeling guilty. He traveled, too, because he had a notion that by visiting a new and strange place he added a little something to his personality. Of course the chief reason he traveled was to get material for writing. Setting is far more important in Maugham's fiction than it is in the fiction of most writers. He specialized in exotic settings—a plantation in the Malay Peninsula, Borneo, India, Samoa, Peking, French Indo-China. He went to Tahiti to get material for *The Moon and Sixpence,* and to India for *The Razor's Edge.* He visited the Caribbean islands because Kipling had told him there were a lot of stories there, though they weren't his sort. (Maugham decided they weren't his sort either.) More often he went simply to gather whatever impressions he could.

Wherever Maugham went, he carried with him as exact a knowledge of the country as he could get from wide reading. In addition, he was gifted with a discriminating intelligence, sensitivity, and a disinterested curiosity about people and places.

He was never deterred by hardship or danger. He loves luxury, but he is not dependent on it. He cheerfully ate hamburgers day after day and slept in native huts or on copra sacks in an open launch when he could do no better. He sailed in unseaworthy ships to remote islands and rode a Shan pony into areas rarely visited by white men.

Unlike the usual traveler, Maugham's interest in a place is not dependent on his encountering anything striking in the way of people or scenery. In fact, he is indifferent to scenery as such. On a motor trip through our western states he missed much of the spectacular scenery because he took a nap in the car every day after lunch.

People are another matter. He is interested in everyone he encounters, and is as fascinated by a dull person as a witty one. He never seeks to impress his personality on others; he doesn't care what you think of him, but is much interested in what he thinks of you. His notebooks suggest a kind of recording machine, which gets down accurately what people look like and say, never intruding his own reactions. He is more interested in people than in places, but he describes places in detail because they have a part in making people what they are. He sorts people into their several categories, and he never exaggerates their traits in order to present them as "characters." He describes physical characteristics and dress, and he usually records nationality and peculiarities of voice.

For all his wide travel, Maugham describes himself as a bad traveler, but he does not expect you to take him at his word. The "good" traveler, he says, is one who is so pleased with his way of doing things that he is childishly delighted by the absurdity of eating with chopsticks or riding in a rickshaw. Everything different is oh-so-quaint for him. Maugham is surprised at nothing, and so adaptable that after a few days he sees nothing strange in writing with a brush or sitting on the floor.

There is hardly a Maugham book, fiction or non-fiction, that does not show the impact of his travels, but only four can be labeled travel books, and one of these, *Don Fernando*, could as well be classified as a series of essays.

The first of the four, *The Land of the Blessed Virgin* (also called *Andalusia*), was published in 1905 and is unimportant. When he wrote it Maugham believed that his natural style was much too plain, and he sought to enrich it with elaborate similes and quaint allusions. Some years ago, at the suggestion of his publisher, he looked it over with the idea of revising it. He put it down with horror.

Of the other three, *Don Fernando* is also about Spain; *On a Chinese Screen* is the fruit of his first trip to China; and *The Gentleman in the Parlour* is a record of a journey from Rangoon to Haiphong. In his published notebooks Maugham has deleted everything that supplied material for these books, presumably because the notes and the books are so much alike. In fact, he tells us that *On a Chinese Screen* is simply the notes, slightly revised.

If we compare the notes with the polished sketches, we see the kind of revision they have undergone. Whereas the notebook entries are simply a collection of sharply observed facts, undramatic and usually without point, each of the sketches in *On a Chinese Screen* has a theme. Most of them are about people, and what always fascinates Maugham about people is their inconsistency. *Chinese Screen* contains sketches of the hard-boiled crook who has a real love of painting and Chinese calligraphy; the missionary who hates his wife and calling; the perfectly ordinary man who has led an extraordinary life; the Socialist who abuses coolies, the missionary who became a successful business man, and then, just as we are beginning to detect the formula, a real shocker: two priests who are good and true servants of God.

Maugham's travel books are his least popular works, chiefly because they are so different from the novels and short stories that gained him his enormous reading public. Many of the faithful, hoping for another *Moon and Sixpence*, rushed to buy *On a Chinese Screen* and were disappointed. They expected a rattling good story in the Maugham manner, but Maugham's skill as a storyteller counts for nothing in these sketches because there is no story to tell. There are none of the melodramatic incidents that thrill most readers of Maugham's stories, and no acid comments on the weakness of women. There is no adultery and, coming from a professed agnostic, entirely too much about God. Maugham is far too serene and compassionate to sound natural.

Nevertheless, for a few readers who like their Maugham unadulterated, these books are the Master at his finest. Before 1922, when *On a Chinese Screen* was published, he had shown himself to be a superb storyteller, but not a great artist. Maugham had always known the force of simple, familiar words, but not until he wrote this book had he learned how to string them together in a seemingly casual, natural order. Although there is hardly a sentence which, lifted out of context, seems remarkable, the effect of the whole is compelling. It is art that conceals art.

But this is not the only merit of the work. In *The Summing Up* Maugham advises the aspiring writer to develop "that idiosyncrasy which may give only a partial picture of the facts, but is suffused by the personality of the observer." *On a Chinese Screen* is the first of his works in which Maugham really put this precept to work. It is positively drenched with Maugham's writing personality, though it is not the first in which he used the first person. *The Moon and Sixpence* is first person, and so are a few of the early short stories. In these the narrator's personality counts for little; he is just someone who tells the story, he is not really a character in it. But in *Chinese Screen* and in many of the stories that follow it, though he never influences the action he is the most important character. We get to know him well.

Maugham's personality as seen in his writing is an impressive work of art, and accounts for much of his popularity. What manner of man is the "I" of his stories? He is a learned man, but we forgive him for it, for with phrases like "as we all know" he implies that we know as much as he does. He is a modest man, embarrassed when the headman of a village in Indo-China greets him with a present of eggs, rice, and bananas. He is only a wandering stranger, and the instructions they have received to make his way easy have misled them into thinking him a person of consequence. He is worldly, and shrewd in his judgment of men and events. He is realistic, he faces the facts, even at the risk of being thought cynical by the sentimentalists. Therefore he can but find men pitifully weak and ignoble, and he is honest enough to say so. He is so tolerant that he makes us ashamed to condemn the ignobility he has made us aware of.

His senses are keen and his heart is compassionate, and he makes them ours by his repeated use of "we" and "you." Therefore it is with his eyes that we see the magical beauty of the hills and valleys at that moment when it is no longer night, but not yet day. It is with his soft heart that we feel for the browbeaten, sweating coolies. Ignorant and earthbound though we are, "the shivering bamboos with their high-bred grace" remind us too of "groups of ladies in the Great Ming dynasty resting languidly by the wayside," and when the Peking cart disappears into the gathering darkness, we too feel that it carries all the mystery of the East.

As we see him in his writing, Maugham is all of this and more. He is independent; he does not give a damn whether we like him or not, and we respect him for it. So do the characters in his stories. He is kindly, understanding, and shock-proof. The worldliness leavened by the kindliness make him an ideal father confessor, and we see why so many of his characters confess to him their sins of murder, theft, incest, and adultery, and why they run to him for help. They beg him to go to Paris to snag a defaulted husband or to Blackstable to get the facts on an adulterous wife. He is always reluctant to go, he likes to mind his own business, but he always goes and he doesn't even ask for carfare.

In short, he is as artful a seducer as ever persuaded readers to buy his books.

Maugham makes more use of his "I" in short stories than in novels. His next novel, *The Painted Veil* (1925), was written in the third person, but one has no difficulty in recognizing the product as vintage Maugham, for it has the familiar Maugham ingredients of a foreign setting, adultery, and God. The novel opens in Hong Kong, and in the first scene Dr. Fane surprises his wife Kitty in bed with her lover. At the moment, Dr. Fane expresses his displeasure only by spookishly turning the doorknob; but in the showdown the lover—a handsome, highly-placed scoundrel with charm—abandons his broken-hearted mistress for a perfectly plain wife, and Kitty, to expiate her sin, is forced to accompany her husband to plague-infested Mei-tan-fu in the interior of China. There the French nuns in the convent effect her regeneration.

The plot of the novel moves along soap-opera lines, but there are incidents likely to confuse soap-opera lovers. When the regenerated Kitty—chastened, widowed, and pregnant—returns to Hong Kong, she meets her ex-lover again and is re-seduced in half a page. At this point Maugham thinks better of his heroine than some of his readers do. She herself is bitterly ashamed, but he implies that her sin is venial and much better behavior can be expected of her in the future.

Like most Maugham stories, this is a good one, but the Maugham theme does not fare so well. Luckily the title supplies a clue, for the plot overshadows the theme. The painted veil is that which obscures reality, and Kitty Fane is one of the many Maugham characters who struggle to grasp and accept reality. Her intellectual improvement is superior to her moral improvement. She comes to understand much that heretofore she was too flibberti-gibbet to comprehend. But, as we have seen, although she sees the light she does not follow it unswervingly.

Walter Fane is a character into whom Maugham poured

much of himself, and, like most of those who resemble their creator, Fane is unattractive, unlovable, and slightly ridiculous. Both Maugham and Fane are men of science. Maugham puts into Fane's mouth the same words he used to describe himself as a bridge player: a very good player of the second class. More significant are the similarities between the characters of the two men.

Like Maugham, Fane is very reserved. Everything his wife found out about his life before she met him, she elicited by direct questioning. As long as I have known him, I have never heard Maugham bring up the subject of his school days, his early life in Paris, the years he spent there following the publication of *Liza*, his extensive travels, or his successes or failures as a writer. He has never mentioned the girl, obviously important in his life, who was the original of Mildred in *Of Human Bondage*. (I once asked him tentatively whether Mildred was drawn from a person he knew, and he said "Yes" in an abrupt tone of voice that shut off that line of inquiry.)

Like Fane, Maugham is self-conscious; neither could possibly bring himself to sing when others are singing. In both, an abnormal degree of self-control holds in check a fiercely passionate nature. Both men have over-perfect manners, which keep others at a distance. Their smiles are forced, a kind of sarcastic smirk which suggests they think most people are fools. They share a disconcerting habit of saying nothing when they have nothing to say. Both lack charm, and that is why, according to Maugham, Walter Fane was not popular in Hong Kong.

Maugham has broadcast his agnosticism so widely that few readers look for evidence of a contrary attitude in his writing. Most take his word for it, and in their eyes he is the devil's disciple if not his co-worker, a mocker and a scoffer who holds nothing sacred. Their notion of Maugham's religious views comes from "Rain," and they reprobate an author who writes a story in which a missionary falls in love with a prostitute, even though at the end he commits suicide by way of atonement.

The fact is that if you go through Maugham's writing— especially *The Painted Veil*—looking for evidence of his religious views, you come up with some unexpected conclusions. True, in his early writing Maugham was angry at God. When Bertha Craddock (*Mrs. Craddock*) and Mrs. Littlewood (*The Unknown*), two women sorely buffeted by fate, are urged to beg God's forgiveness for blaspheming against Him, both ask ringingly, "And who is going to forgive God?" Later Maugham's attitude softened. For one who professes disbelief, he refers to the Deity with surprising frequency, always implying that he and God are on the best of terms. His God, of course, is not everybody's God. He is a well-bred upper-class English gentleman with a sense of humor, rather like an Oxford man who graduated with a first. Like Maugham, He is embarrassed if you praise Him to His face. He is a trifle worldly and remarkably tolerant of sin, especially adultery.

Maugham's attitude toward missionaries is not nearly so intolerant as it is supposed to be. He did not love them, he was shocked by their use of economic means to gain spiritual ends, but he was fair to them. There is only one Davidson and there are many virtuous missionaries. Maugham praises their virtues while deploring their manners.

What is clear, if you look for the evidence, is that he admired and respected the Roman Catholic Church. The Protestant missionary and the Catholic priest are different breeds of men. The missionaries in "The Stranger" go to the hills for the hot summer months, but the priests remain in the sweltering city. Maugham's pages abound with selfless priests, kindly, good-natured nuns, and grave Mothers Superior with exquisite manners whose air of authority is tempered by Christian charity. The Protestant bishops are often self-seeking hypocrites, but the Catholic bishops are like their Church: wise, kind, and tolerant. It is Elliott Templeton's Catholicism, not the Catholic Church, that is satirized in *The Razor's Edge*.

Despite his professed agnosticism Maugham, I think, yearns to believe in God, especially now that he is old and within hailing distance of death. Three obstacles stand in his way: first, his skeptical, rational turn of mind. He has read everything on the subject and finds no proof of the existence of God that satisfies his intellect. Second, his keen sense of irony. The near-deathbed conversion of the well-publicized agnostic is a spectacle he enjoys only when someone else plays the leading role. For himself, fidelity to one's principles is more becoming. Third, the feeling that conversion at this point is nothing but a cowardly fear of what lies ahead. And he is well acquainted with the argument that it is only his pride that stands in his way.

Nevertheless, I think he is ripe for conversion to Roman Catholicism. I once expressed this view to a Catholic friend who said he would pass it along and perhaps the Church might extend a hand to the sinner. Whether it did or not, I do not know.

In 1928, having had his fill of travel for the time being, Maugham bought a house at Cap Ferrat, a neck of land that stretches out into the Mediterranean between Nice and Monte Carlo on the French Riviera. The Villa Mauresque was built at the beginning of the century by a retired Catholic bishop who had lived most of his life in Algeria. It had a Moorish cupola, horseshoe windows, a Moorish archway across the living room, and a Renaissance loggia, and was so hideous, Maugham says, that no one else wanted it and he got it cheap. It occurred to him that all this Moorish nonsense and Renaissance exuberance were only lath and plaster, and could be scraped away to leave a plain house with a flat roof.

After the house was remodeled Maugham moved in and surrounded himself with luxury—liveried servants, a yacht, a swimming pool, paintings by Matisse and Renoir, and motor cars by Rolls-Royce and Voisin. Chattels like these stimulate his imagination, he says, as they did Rembrandt's, but they are unimportant to his spirit's well-being, and he could give them all up without a pang if he had to. Like his good friend the late Aga Khan, Maugham has had the best of two worlds.

Maugham added a writing room to the house, so isolated that you have to cross a stretch of open roof to get to it.

The room is on the Mediterranean side, and when I first saw it I remarked that it might have provided a magnificent view of the sea below. Maugham said that it had originally, but the view distracted him and he removed the window which looked on it.

The room is not especially large. On several sides there are bookshelves, and there is a lectern on which Maugham can place a reference book. When the Villa Mauresque was full of guests (it isn't nowadays), Maugham could work in his writing room in peace. Only a bold man would venture there uninvited.

There are twelve acres of land around the Villa Mauresque, and Maugham planted oleanders, camellias, and other flowering shrubs, and imported avocado trees from California. These bore no fruit for seven years, but when World War II forced him to flee, Maugham was getting several hundred pears a year, the first to be grown in Europe. He says his greatest luxury is grass because, the summer being too hot for it, it has to be replanted every spring. Maugham likens its fresh young green to the look in a young girl's eyes at her first ball.

Shortly after he settled into the Villa Mauresque, *Cakes and Ale* was published. It is Maugham's favorite among his novels and is about as perfect as its kind of novel can be. The plot is slight; the narrator's way of telling the story and his soliloquies and asides give the book its unique flavor. This narrator is not quite the same gentleman we got to know so well in the short stories and the travel books. The compassionate Maugham has temporarily retired from the scene, and the satirist has taken over. He is all brain and no heart. His style is witty and urbane, casual and digressive, but his aim is deadly and he annihilates his target. You feel he is malicious and wickedly unfair, but you admire Maugham's skill and you relish every page of this short novel.

Cakes and Ale followed the same pattern Maugham used in *The Moon and Sixpence* and would use again in *The Razor's Edge.* The hero of each novel is a striking personality, a genius of sorts, and the narrator, a person everyone confides in, happens to know him. The narrator is busy leading his own life, but fortunately for us his path and the hero's cross at just the right moments for him to learn all he needs to know in order to interpret the hero for us.

Writing the novel presented many technical problems, and Maugham said he enjoyed solving them. There are two stories: the story of the narrator, Ashenden, and his relations with Alroy Kear and Mrs. Driffield, and the story of Edward and Rosie Driffield. The first story moves in the present; the second begins forty years before and comes up to the present. The problem was how to weave the two stories into one smooth-flowing narrative. Maugham solved it by the use of the flashback, a device much used today. Jerome Weidman gives Maugham credit for being the first to employ it in a novel.

Cakes and Ale stirred up more controversy than all the other Maugham books put together. Maugham must have known that it would; he said he wrote it with great glee.

No sooner was it published than the critics identified Edward Driffield with Thomas Hardy, and Alroy Kear with Hugh Walpole. Neither character is exactly heroic.

Maugham has never admitted he had Hardy in mind when he drew Driffield. According to him, the critics saw Hardy in Driffield only because Hardy had died shortly before the novel appeared. He says Driffield resembles Hardy no more than he does Meredith or Tennyson. Of course this is nonsense. Tennyson was a poet, Driffield a novelist, and there is no similarity between the two men's characters. What rules out Meredith and clinches Hardy is that what the critics in Maugham's novel say of Driffield is just what Hardy's critics said of him.

Maugham told me that the original of Driffield was an unimportant writer whom he had known in Whitstable when he was a boy. The theme of the novel, he added, is the contrast between the man whom the world sees and the real man within. All this is, no doubt, true, but it does not preclude the possibility that he was also portraying Hardy.

Though Hardy was dead and his battle had to be fought by others, Walpole was very much alive when the novel appeared, and he had no doubt that he had sat for the portrait of Kear. (He once signed a letter "not Alroy Kear but HUGH WALPOLE!") He sent Maugham a hurt, sorrowful note. Maugham replied with wide-eyed innocence that he hadn't had Walpole in mind at all, how could he think such a thing? Certain unpleasant traits, he said, are common to all writers, and that was why Walpole saw himself in Kear. The really nasty parts of Kear, he claimed, came from himself.

In my opinion, there is not much Maugham in Alroy Kear, but at least one incident involving Kear, which shows him as a self-seeking hypocrite, came from Maugham's own experience. When in the novel someone wrote a stinging criticism of one of his books, Kear wrote a letter thanking the critic for his penetrating criticism and asking him to lunch so that he might further profit by the critic's insight. The critic came, Kear was a good host, and the lunch was excellent; somehow when Kear's next book appeared, the critic found it to be a very great advance.

We were not discussing *Cakes and Ale* at the time, and I doubt that Maugham recalled he had used the incident in the novel, but he once told me that he had handled an American critic in exactly that way.

Cakes and Ale ruined Walpole's reputation as a writer and embittered the last eleven years of his life. Whatever doubts Walpole may have had, his ill-advised strategy was to accept Maugham's assurance that he was not the original of Kear and to remain on terms of friendship with him. He went so far as to attack the novelist who wrote a novel attacking Maugham for writing *Cakes and Ale*. He accepted Maugham's invitation to a large dinner party at Claridge's to celebrate the birth of his granddaughter, where his presence aroused much mirth among the literati, for although Walpole may have accepted Maugham's word that he was not the original of Kear, no one else did.

After Walpole's death, Maugham admitted that he had had Walpole in mind. A writer has to start with somebody when he draws a character, he said, and he thought he had covered his tracks. When Rupert Hart-Davis' biography of Walpole appeared, he read it, pronounced it good, and maintained that it demonstrated that he had told the absolute truth. He wasn't cruel at all, he said. Walpole was an awful person, as mean as cat's meat.

I have a notion Maugham intended Alroy Kear to be recognized as Hugh Walpole. Maugham may have despised Walpole, but he would not attack him in print for that reason. There would have to be something personal. I gathered that he disliked Walpole, for he kept a tight-lipped silence whenever his name was mentioned. The only reference he ever made in my hearing was that he found Walpole's novels unreadable. Maugham also disliked Henry James, and there may be a connection between his dislike of the two men. In 1914 James wrote an article in the *Times Literary Supplement* called "The Younger Novelists." There were eight of them. Walpole, a close friend of James, was one. Maugham wasn't.

The Driffield–Hardy, Kear–Walpole controversy has spotlighted these characters and thrown others into shadow. Maugham's favorite character in the novel is Rosie. He said he once proposed—what, he did not say— to the girl who was the original of Rosie. She is truly a charming girl, unspoiled and remarkably generous. Like many Maugham heroines, she fornicates at the drop of a hat, yet nevertheless retains her essential purity and innocence.

A year after *Cakes and Ale* appeared, a New York publisher brought out a novel called *Gin and Bitters*, by "A. Riposte." Its dust cover describes it as "a novel about a novelist who writes novels about other novelists." "A. Riposte" was Elinor Mordaunt, and the book is a personal, vindictive attack on Maugham. The author seems to have followed in Maugham's footsteps in Tahiti and other South Sea islands, and collected everything unpleasant about him that she could. Her Leverson Hurle is a monster, quite unlike the far more complex original, but clearly it is Maugham she is attacking.

Maugham professed surprise and lofty indifference. He was, in fact, far from indifferent. Gerald Haxton told me he somehow got hold of the page proof of the book before it was published, and the two of them sat up all one night feverishly reading it. When they had finished, Maugham decided he would not sue the publisher for libel, for if he did, he would only puff a mediocre work into a *succès de scandale*. Maugham was not, however, above threatening to sue, and he took steps to suppress the novel in England. *Gin and Bitters* sold three thousand copies and owes its slight fame to its subject rather than to merit.

CHAPTER 5 ⚔⚔

The Man Behind the Mask

I ONCE asked Maugham whether the "I" of his stories was supposed to be himself. He said yes, but it wasn't a complete portrait. That was an understatement. The "I" of the stories is not only not the real Maugham, he is but a character fashioned to serve as a teller of tales. And the "I" of the non-fiction is likewise a fictional character.

Of course there is a similarity between the real Maugham and the character who impersonates him, which explains why people who are introduced to him often have the startled feeling that they have met him before. But the "I" of the books is synthetic Maugham, purged of impurities, contradictions and inconsistencies, and glazed with charm.

The differences between the two Maughams are many. Take the matter of charm. The "I" has it and Maugham lacks it, and is well aware that he does. He is too cold, too studied and self-conscious to be charming. He hasn't the physical assets that are a part of it—a pleasing exterior or a fetching ugliness. He knows that his fame rather than any warmth of personality attracts people to him, and he is sardonically amused by the fact. He candidly admits that many people find his personality odious. Nevertheless, his is an impressive personality, which would attract attention had he never written a line. Without knowing who he was, you might well turn to look at him a second time, just as you would look twice at Satan.

Or take the matter of consistency. The narrator is always true to type: even-tempered, genially caustic, aloof yet kindly, as predictable as rain in the tropics. Maugham is all of these when the fit is on, but it isn't always on. A careful reader of his books might guess this, for one theme runs through almost everything he wrote: man is a bundle of contradictions, and only a fool thinks he knows what his best friend will do next. This is a truth which Maugham had only to look within himself to discover, for he is as inconsistent and unpredictable as they come. He is cynical and sentimental, serene and irritable, an agnostic who has a yen to believe in God, a fastidious, upper-class gentleman who thinks the lower classes should and will inherit the earth, an abnormally reticent man who in *Of Human Bondage* and *The Summing Up* broadcast some embarrassingly intimate details of his life, a kindly, tolerant person who can be caustic and cruel without warning or provocation.

Maugham himself has long been aware of the inconsistency. At twenty-two he jotted down in his notebook, "There are times when I look over the various parts of my character with perplexity. I recognise that I am made up of several persons and that the person which at the moment has the upper hand will inevitably give place to another. But which is the real me? All of them or none?"

Anyone who attempts to discover the real Maugham will get no help from the gentleman himself. For the real Maugham lives behind a wall of reserve which few persons have ever breached. His essential self is as remote and impenetrable as the Malayan jungle he wrote about. That complete and perfect intimacy with another human being which many regard as the crown of life fills him with horror.

Several suits of armor protect the inner man from the probes of the curious. One is his Chesterfieldian elegance and breeding, which hold people at arm's length. He can be at the same time as genial as Arthur Godfrey and as inaccessible as Mt. Everest. His manners are so polished that his speech and actions provide small clue to his thoughts.

Another suit of armor is his acting ability. "The celebrated develop a technique to deal with the persons they come across," he wrote in *The Summing Up*. "They show the world a mask, often an impressive one, but take care to conceal their real selves. They play the part that is expected from them and with practice learn to play it very well, but you are stupid if you think that this public performance of theirs corresponds with the man within."

Any attempt to understand Maugham must take into account three factors: his stammer, his short stature, and his incredible will power. The first two forced him to introspection and shaped the view of his fellow man that gives his stories their unique quality. The third enabled him to make the most of his talent and to revamp his personality according to his whim. For without taking issue with his favorite thesis that man is a bundle of contradictions, I find another reason why Maugham is a bigger bundle than most.

Maugham's is a reconstructed personality. He was born one kind of person and by an act of will made himself into another. Dissatisfied with what God and his parents had wrought, he effected an improvement. The mature Maugham is the youthful Maugham's ideal, or a reasonably good facsimile, the best he could fashion from the raw materials at hand. The ideal he sought was perfectly realized only in the "I" of his writing. But he succeeded to a surprising extent in remodeling himself. He is by nature irritable, suspicious, and easily affronted. These and other defects of character he was early aware of, and determined to eradicate. Maugham, who takes people as he finds them and is amused by those who seek to improve them, sought earnestly to improve himself. His serenity, charity, and indifference to the opinions of others are not a pose. They are an attitude of mind he has almost made his own. He is himself a work of art, a character as carefully contrived and as plausible as any of his fictional characters. And, like them, he sometimes behaves out of character. That is why a story about him in which he appears, let us say, charitable and humane can often be matched by another which shows him to be caustic and cruel.

Here are several stories to illustrate my point. Maugham's cultivated manner is an almost Buddhistic calm. He will not allow himself to be irritated by situations which infuriate most of us. But I recall a time when we were dining in the Oak Room of the Plaza in New York. We were going to the theatre and so kept an eye on the clock. Maugham ordered green turtle soup, and when it hadn't arrived ten minutes later he began to fidget. Ten minutes after that he burst out in fury.

"This is absurd! I shall speak to the head waiter!"

Maugham was seated against the wall. I was on the outside.

"D'you want me to?"

"No, I want to myself!" He shoved the table aside and started to get up. The head waiter glided swiftly forward.

"Where is our dinner?"

"But Mr. Maugham, you ordered turtle soup. Turtle soup has to be made."

"Stuff and nonsense. All you do is open a can."

"Oh no, Mr. Maugham. It is fresh turtle soup."

The soup materialized and Maugham was served. With two waiters hovering anxiously over him he took a loud sip. He smacked his lips.

"Very good. Very good indeed." The waiters sighed and faded away.

On another occasion, with far greater provocation, Maugham behaved with Christian forbearance. A magazine had bought an article I had written about him, and sent a photographer to his home to take pictures. I happened to be visiting Maugham at the time. Maugham graciously invited the man to lunch and afterwards, forgoing his usual nap, allowed himself to be photographed in a dozen poses. When this was over, the man showed no signs of leaving. I became uneasy, but Maugham remained calm and cheerful. The afternoon passed, our visitor still remained, and Maugham invited him to dinner. Throughout the meal the host was courteous and affable. After dinner the man showed snapshots and told us all about his unhappy childhood. Finally, about midnight, he seemed about to leave. I was on my feet in a flash. Maugham arose slowly and escorted his guest to the door. He bade him a polite farewell and carefully closed the door. Nervously I awaited the onslaught, for I felt that in a way I was responsible.

"He does pay long calls, doesn't he?" Maugham said mildly. "And I had hoped we could have some canasta."

Maugham's exemplary behavior in this trying situation could be attributed to his sensitivity to the feelings of others, and I know many examples of it. One of them involves another photographer. We were dining at the Brown Derby in Hollywood, and the photographer came up to our table.

"Good evening, Mr. Maugham. May I take your picture?"

"Certainly, if you like."

"Just go right on talking."

This was easy for Maugham, who was used to this sort of thing, but I froze. Maugham saw what had happened and spoke casually.

"This is the time I always recite the Lord's Prayer."

"Our Father . . ." I began timidly.

"Who art in heaven," continued Maugham in a firm voice.

"Hallowed be Thy name." The photographer snapped the picture and we went on with our dinner.

A few years later I reminded Maugham of this incident and he said he had tried the same thing with Fannie Hurst, but she didn't seem to know the Lord's Prayer and was under the impression he was talking about one of his own compositions.

Maugham's rented home in Beverly Hills was the scene of a far more embarrassing incident, and again his sensitivity to my feelings spared me. We were driving home from a party in an Oldsmobile he had just bought. Maugham isn't a good driver, for until the war he had always had a chauffeur. The garage was difficult to get into, for you had to turn sharply just before entering. When we reached this point Maugham stopped the car and asked me whether I could put it in the garage.

"Oh yes," I said confidently.

"It's a new car, you know."

"It's no trick at all."

We changed seats, I put the car in gear, and we started forward. There was a sickening crunch of metal and the car went in—with a bashed fender.

Throughout the ordeal Maugham sat silent and unperturbed. When the last deafening echo had died away and I was too humiliated to speak, he said lightly, "I could have done that well myself."

But just as many stories illustrate a lordly disregard for the feelings of others, even a slight waspishness. Bridge is a serious business in Maugham's life, and when he sits down at the bridge table he will brook no nonsense. On one occasion one of the players was a woman who had met Maugham for the first time that day. She chattered without stopping. After ten minutes Maugham slammed his cards on the table.

"If we're going to play cards," he said firmly, "you'll have to keep your mouth shut."

At another bridge game he took out a cigar. His partner intimated that she didn't care for cigar smoke and would really rather that he didn't smoke it.

"I'm sorry you don't like it," Maugham said apologetically. "But I intend to smoke it anyway."

Cigars, like bridge, Maugham takes very seriously, and his friends know it. Once he was dining at the New York apartment of Richard Simon, the publisher. Just before he was due to arrive, Simon, realizing with consternation that he hadn't a cigar in the place, rushed out to the nearest cigar store and bought a supply of their best. After dinner he offered the box to Maugham, who adjusted his monocle and, picking up one, carefully noted the brand.

"No thanks," he said, putting it back and taking a cigar out of his pocket.

Maugham ordinarily disdains cheap wit. But how does one explain the Hartley incident? The scene was an after-theatre party in London. Among the guests were Gladys Cooper, the charming actress who played the feminine lead in the London productions of a number of Maugham's plays, and a well-known actor whom I shall call David Hartley because that isn't his name. In the course of the evening Mr. Hartley sauntered over to Maugham.

"Willie," he said, "you always write such marvelous parts for Gladys. Why don't you write a part for me?"

"I have, David," said Willie. "I've written many parts for you. But Gladys always plays them."

Maugham's ideal state of mind is an aloofness of spirit which nothing mundane can disturb. He likes to feel he is completely indifferent to what others think of him or his writing. But the man underneath is remarkably thin-skinned. When a Hollywood gossip columnist reported that he was taking driving lessons, he stopped them immediately. He does not read reviews of his books. He says he learns nothing from them, but I suspect he doesn't read them because derogatory criticism upsets him. Various small incidents point to a tender hide. Years ago I asked Maugham to read an article I had written about him, to make sure I had said nothing that might embarrass him. He replied loftily that nothing would embarrass him, absolutely nothing, and I could say whatever I pleased. The article appeared. I doubt very much that he read it; at any rate, there were no repercussions.

Then the editor suggested I write a second article on Maugham, this one describing his luxurious gourmet life and including a recipe or two for the food served in his home. I didn't know Maugham then as well as I do now and so I happily wrote him, confident that he would approve and assist. I got back a blast I shall never forget. The article, he said, would make him look ridiculous. There was nothing unusual about the way he lived, every gentleman lived the same way, and his food was no better than anyone else's who took a little trouble. I could write the article if I liked, but I would get no help from him. He also thanked me for a fishing rod I had sent him.

Once when he was living in this country during the war, his friend Jerome Weidman happened to meet him on the street.

"Hello, Willie. I hear you've been in Hollywood."

"Yes, and I was a failure there."

"You a failure? That's not what I heard."

"Yes. You're a failure in Hollywood unless you're invited to Mrs. Jack Warner's, and I wasn't invited." Maugham made a joke of it, but it was clear that the slight rankled.

Maugham has often been called a cynic. Whether you think he is or not depends upon your notion of cynicism, for one man's cynicism is another man's realism. The epithet was hurled at Maugham early in his career and it stuck. Maugham puts his answer into the mouth of one of his characters: "If to look truth in the face and not resent it when it's unpalatable, and take human nature as you find it, smiling when it's absurd and grieved without exaggeration when it's pitiful, is to be cynical, then I suppose I'm a cynic." Written in 1931, this is a fair statement of his mature attitude. But the Maugham of the early work is a different animal. He did not resent unpalatable truth or grieve over it; he embraced it gleefully.

When he grew older and set himself up as a serious student of human nature, Maugham resented the label, with its implication of frivolity and superficiality, and perhaps he no longer deserved it. The gleeful tone has been muted, but he continues to cast a cold clinical eye on what others call virtue. I remember his remarking that one of the facts of human nature which people simply will not accept is that no man wants to sleep with the same woman all his life. When he makes such an observation, Maugham's manner of speaking is as matter of fact as if he were bidding two spades, and he manages to imply that those who disagree are hypocrites or sentimentalists or both.

The label of cynic is so firmly attached that few realize Maugham has a streak of sentimentality in him. One day, after he had read a pile of fan letters that had arrived in the daily mail, he said sadly, "All those letters and nothing from a friend."

You would not think Maugham could be humbled by anything, but when he encounters that "most precious and loveliest" of all qualities—goodness—he is awed into reverence. Love he has little respect for. However much we resent the fact and angrily deny it, love, he says, depends on certain secretions of the sexual glands. But not goodness. Goodness cannot be analyzed, accounted for, or explained away. It is the indivisible element in human nature. There is very little of it in the world, but the fisherman Salvatore had it and you can find it in priests.

I think Maugham despises the vein of sentimentality in himself as he despises it in others, for while the fit is on his emotions rule his intellect and he sees life out of focus. Sentimentality in others so revolts him that when he encounters it he invariably sounds off with something harshly realistic—or cynical. This may explain a remark he once made, a remark which his hearers found callous and offensive. He was having lunch with two women friends who were deploring a tragedy in the life of a mutual friend. They told Maugham that their friend's adolescent daughter had suddenly died, and overnight her hair had become streaked with gray. Maugham snorted.

"It's more likely she couldn't make her regular visit to the beauty parlor."

Maugham's conduct, when it isn't out of control, is governed by his concept of what is fitting behavior for a gentleman. Maugham's kind of gentleman does not grow on gooseberry bushes; he is a five-generation phenomenon, almost extinct in these egalitarian times. Maugham is aware that his ideal is no longer universally admired, and he explains it thus: "Persons who by no stretch of the fancy could be so described have made a great stir in the world for the last thirty years and they have used all the resources of their sarcasm to render odious a title which they are perhaps all too conscious of never deserving."

The gentleman lives by a code, in Maugham's case an austere one which imposes an iron discipline on his occasionally frivolous impulses. He is generous, modest, and noblesse-obliging. He is courteous, frank, and kind to dumb animals. These virtues are no less real for being not spontaneous but consciously cultivated. Only the innately virtuous desire to act virtuously, and only the strong-willed among them succeed. Maugham belongs to this category.

He is generous in subtle ways. He will repeat to others a clever remark you have made and praise your wit. If you tell him what he already knows, he does not interrupt you but listens to you without impatience. He says that people like to tell what they know, it is a harmless pastime, why not indulge it?

He gives liberally not only of his money, which perhaps he can well afford, but also of his time and energy. When he is in the mood he will go to endless trouble to help someone he hardly knows. He is accessible to aspiring young writers who send him their manuscripts and beg his advice. If the novel is promising, he takes infinite pains.

There is, of course, a story which shows him to be just the opposite of all this. A New York publishing house was bringing out a first novel by a writer they thought highly of, and an editor who knows Maugham sent him an advance copy with the request that he write a few kind words which might appear on the dust cover, if he liked the novel. This kind of request is routine, and established writers far less amiable and generous than Maugham regularly accede to it.

When the novel arrived, the regenerate Maugham was in temporary eclipse and the base Maugham in the ascendancy. He sent back a blast to the effect that he positively and absolutely refused to do any such thing, or even to read the novel. He said he was sick and tired of young writers trying to climb onto the backs of their betters. The editor was dumfounded. Maugham's shell is so perfect one forgets that under it is a capricious, often irritable human being who sometimes savagely bursts the seams.

Maugham appears to be a modest man. He never implies that he knows better than you and he never tries to bring you around to his way of thinking. He doesn't mind in the least if you disagree with him completely. When you say something he agrees with, he doesn't say, "You are absolutely right," he says, "I think so too." When he disagrees with what you say, he says, "Yes." This means he heard you.

He never demands the center of the stage, and he listens more than he talks. He rarely mentions his writing unless you ask him about it, and then he seems to talk about it only because it would be impolite not to. When he has to refer to one of his books, he is more likely to say what's bad than what's good about it. He will say, "When I wrote a book called *The Narrow Corner . . .*" not, "When I wrote *The Narrow Corner . . .*" for the latter would imply he thought you should know the novel.

Though he claims he will unblushingly take advantage of his renown to get a better cabin on a ship than he has paid for, I have seen him refuse to trade on it. Once I accompanied him to a federal office in Los Angeles, where he had to go on business relating to his visitor's visa. I was surprised that he stood patiently in line for an hour and waited his turn, when he could easily have made known who he was and got the preferred treatment which our democratic officials reserve for the celebrated.

On the other hand, he has no false modesty. He will not, for example, belittle one of his stories in order to appear modest. When I asked him what he thought of the movie of "The Letter," he said he thought it good where it followed his story, bad where it didn't. He said the same thing of the movie hacked out of *The Moon and Sixpence*. Once he told me that although he sold his stories to the

ugham in his
iting room at the
la Mauresque

Entrance to the Villa Mauresque, with Maugham mono-
gram over the door

Maugham sitting [b]
his portrait as a [
man

On the yacht *Sara*

movies when he could, he never went to see the result; remarks dropped at other times make clear that this isn't so. Once I said I thought "The Door of Opportunity" would make an excellent movie, and he replied that he had been telling Hollywood that for years.

Some people who know him say Maugham is conceited, but it may be that words like "modest" and "conceited" are inapplicable to him. He knows how to appear modest whether he really is or not, and he knows how to avoid giving the impression of conceit if he wants to take the trouble, just as he knows the commercial value of his mysterious and slightly sinister personality.

Maugham does not, like his ideal gentleman, despise money and trust God to provide it. He has a phenomenal capacity for earning it and a healthy respect for what he has earned. He knows that he who pays the piper calls the tune, and although he likes yachts and paintings and swimming pools, he likes most of all to call the tune.

He lives in the grand manner, but he has never spent a cent he couldn't well afford. He is openhanded yet thrifty; he knows exactly what he pays for things. At a big dinner party in his home he once told the glittering assembly that the fish course was the most expensive, and said exactly what he paid for it.

He never forgets what it was like to be poor and he never lets you spend more on him than you can afford. When I took him out to dinner, he always insisted on going to a cheaper place than he regularly patronized. When we played bridge he was indifferent to his own financial outcome, but he was concerned how much I had won or lost. He was delighted when after visiting him for a week, thanks to bridge winnings I left with more money than I had when I arrived.

He doesn't often mention money, but when he does he talks like the very rich, not those who have only a million or two. I remember a story he told me about Mrs. Nelson Doubleday and her sister. The girls, Maugham said, hadn't a penny in their own name and their father would give them nothing. Though both women were married to wealthy men and weren't exactly in want, Maugham thought it too bad they hadn't a little pin money of their own. It wasn't, he continued, as if their father couldn't well afford it. He was quite a rich man. "Why," said Maugham, "if he only gave them a million each it would help."

In "Augustus," after describing a manner of life involving cooks, butlers, and parlour maids, dinners of soup, fish, poultry or game, a sweet and a savoury, and a cottage on the estate for the entertainment of gentlewomen in reduced circumstances, Maugham remarks, "Such was a day in one of the smaller country houses at the end of the nineteenth century, and such, more or less, throughout the land was the day in hundreds upon hundreds of houses belonging to persons who, without being rich, were well enough off to live in the great comfort which they looked upon as the way in which gentlefolk should live."

Maugham's persistent gentility has left its mark on his work. No other writer makes half so many references to the social class of his characters. No other writer has drawn half so many characters who are not quite gentlemen. Maugham always implies that nothing could matter less —but he always brings it up. It is his touchstone for explaining human beings. He once accounted for the marital difficulties of *Main Street's* Dr. and Mrs. Kennicott on the grounds that she is a lady, he not quite a gentleman. He wasn't sure whether Sinclair Lewis realized this or not.

The vantage point from which Maugham views others' social position is exalted, but he is affable and understanding and never blames one for not living up to ideals of conduct not a part of one's heritage. The head of the Intelligence Department, he tells us in *Ashenden,* had only one weakness: Having never come in contact with persons of any social importance, when in his new job he met brilliant, beautiful, and distinguished women, he was unduly dazzled. The reason he had never before met persons of social consequence was that he had been only an army colonel.

Much of the time the writer Maugham is at odds with the gentleman. The writer wants to live life with gusto, to experience its every form and variety, to sin and savor sin. The gentleman has always disdained a bohemian existence, he tires easily, he is finicky, he prefers to study his fellow man from the balcony of his suite at Shepheard's. He will endure hardship and danger without complaint, but it is only to sweeten the luxury of a Raffles hotel he will come to at the end of the road. Maugham is interested in the average man. He says he is more concerned with the obscure than with the famous, for the obscure are more often themselves. Concerned he is, but most of his spare time is spent with the famous. In London, San Francisco, or Bangkok, he always dines with the best people.

For although the spirit is strong, the flesh is weak: Maugham has no talent for excess. He gets sick before he can get drunk. As a sinner he has always been more conscientious than voluptuary. And so the gentleman usually wins out. It is at the Ritz, the theatre, and in the homes of the wealthy that Maugham pursues most of his researches into the behavior of people. He is more at ease with a duchess than a ditchdigger. He tries to understand the ditchdigger, for he is often bored and dissatisfied with the gentleman's limited view of life. But he is constitutionally incapable of seeing life from a Steinbeck's angle. He could never draw a Lennie Small or a George Milton. But perhaps the score is even. For neither could Steinbeck draw an Elliott Templeton.

No reader of Maugham's books needs to be told that he has a keen sense of humor. He does not, however, talk like a witty character in one of his plays. He seldom makes a wisecrack, perhaps because the stammer might ruin it. But I recall one fine example. He, Gerald Haxton, and I were passing the time of day, and Gerald told a story about a well-known writer who often visited Maugham in the company of a lady not his wife. At intervals the lady was turned in for a new model, and she was brought along. After one of the visits the discarded number, learning that Maugham had received her successor, wrote him in great indignation.

"Willie was furious when he read that letter," Gerald said.

"What did he do?"

"Oh, he wrote back something to the effect that he was still master in his own house."

"Even if she was no longer mistress in hers," added Willie.

Most of Maugham's humor has a sardonic turn. He is amused by incidents which show people in an absurd, pretentious, or hypocritical light. Once he remarked that people seem to know their friends only by their bad qualities. He said that when he selected the attractive traits of the people he used as models, none of their friends recognized them; but if he made use of an unattractive trait, a dozen people identified the original.

Maugham is also pleased by the lack of pretentiousness in people you might expect to be pretentious. Once he dined at a grand house near Los Angeles, and after dinner the hostess and guests sat on an expensive terrace which overlooked a forest of oil derricks.

"What a shame those derricks are there," said one guest languidly. "They ruin your view."

"Do you think so?" replied the lady of the house. "I rather like them. If they weren't there, I wouldn't be here."

Maugham has the rare faculty of being able to see himself as his worst enemy sees him. In *The Gentleman in the Parlour* he recounts an incident which took place during his travels in Siam. One night his party camped in a spot where few white men had ever been, and he was asked whether two little boys might be brought to have a look at him. They took a look and then, Maugham says, "They were promptly carried away screaming with terror at the revolting sight."

He can even see humor in connection with his own death. There is a story that through someone's carelessness he was sent a copy of the obituary a leading newspaper had prepared against the day when it will be needed. Maugham read it, made a few corrections of fact, and returned it to the editor with these words, "Mild, very mild indeed."

Once when I stayed with him in France a crew of photographers from *Life* magazine arrived and took many pictures of him and of his home. Only two or three have appeared, and I asked Maugham if he knew why.

"I suspect they are keeping them until I die," he replied. "It will be quite a scoop."

Although a woman who has known him for many years told me that he knows absolutely nothing about women (by which she meant that he doesn't draw them as they see themselves), it seems to me that his knowledge of female psychology is astounding. This was brought home to me by an incident that took place in South Carolina. Maugham and I had called at the Doubleday plantation house at a time when Mr. and Mrs. Carlos Kelly were house guests there. Mrs. Kelly is Mrs. Doubleday's sister, and in the course of the conversation it transpired that the sisters were driving to Charleston the next day. I wanted to go to Charleston, and on the way back to Maugham's house I asked him whether it would be all right for me to ask them to take me along.

"You can if you like," Maugham replied. "But I wouldn't if I were you. Tomorrow's going to be the only opportunity those women will have to talk about their husbands, and if you go along they can't do it."

I do not know what Maugham thinks of many important writers. His remarks to me were informal and random. They usually referred to a particular book we had both read, and most were in answer to questions I put to him. Consequently, what he had to say of Hemingway or Marquand or Eliot did not necessarily apply to the total output of these gentlemen. Maugham is more likely to dwell on a writer's defects than on his merits, but that does not mean he is unaware of the merits or unwilling to acknowledge them.

Although casually delivered, Maugham's judgments are not haphazardly arrived at. They seem to have been carefully thought out before he expresses them and to be right on tap when called for. In fact, I often had the disconcerting feeling that he had used the same words before. No doubt he sometimes had, for I wasn't the first person to ask him what he thought of, say, Thomas Wolfe. I suspect he was ready with his answer the first time the question was put to him, and that he took into account that what he said would be repeated.

Once he has formed an opinion of a writer or a book he seldom changes it. I recall only one whom he rated differently on different occasions. She is a woman writer, a friend of his, and he may have been speaking of her as a friend rather than as a writer. Once he described her to me as extremely amusing. Another time he said she was a damned bore. When *For Whom the Bell Tolls* was published, he commented privately—and his comment was widely repeated and resented—that the novel is twice too long. Many years later, in an interview, he acknowledged that Hemingway is a first-class novelist, but I doubt very much that he has changed his opinion of *For Whom the Bell Tolls.*

Maugham's is a judicial mind. He is not given to reckless enthusiasm or wholesale condemnations. He is bored by many books, but the only one I ever heard him express violent dislike of is Adler's *How to Read a Book.* He wrote me that he had read it with profound disagreement but he hadn't the energy to tell me all the ill he thought of it. That must wait until we met. A book which delighted him more than most was Professor Kinsey's first volume, which his friend Glenway Wescott sent him.

Maugham weighs every book and every person in the balance and finds most of them wanting. But his manner of expressing his opinions is so well-bred, his disparagement so moderately phrased, his point so seemingly sensible, that it is only later that you realize that practically all of them are derogatory. The only writer he mentioned whom he didn't disparage in some way was Jerome Weidman, and that may have been because we didn't pursue the subject. It certainly wasn't merely because Weidman is a good friend. We were talking about my writing at the time, and Maugham said that if I wanted to learn to write a really good colloquial style, I should study Weidman's writing.

Sometimes there was a left-handed compliment wrapped up with a crack, as when he said that Mencken talked well in a bitter sort of way. (Mencken didn't go overboard for Maugham either. He once wrote me that Maugham had written a lot of worthless books as well as some good ones, but he added, "Who of us hasn't?") John Van Druten, Maugham said, had succeeded as a dramatist with the least possible talent. It was a triumph of character, and John deserved a lot of credit.

This remark was tossed off just before Van Druten arrived for lunch. Wherever I visited Maugham—in New York, California, South Carolina, Washington, or France —an endless procession of people came to lunch and dinner, and before they were due, Maugham would give me a thumbnail sketch of those I hadn't met. Some of these vignettes were really hair-raising. One in particular I recall.

It was at the Villa Mauresque, and an old and valued friend was bringing a woman friend to dinner. Maugham said they were trying out marriage to decide whether they wanted to make it legal. His friend, Maugham said, was kind, thoughtful, generous. He would give you the shirt off his back. He was also intelligent, rich, and public-spirited. In fact, said our host, his friend was absolutely tops in practically every way. Maugham paused dramatically, then added, "It also happens that he is a complete son of a bitch."

Before Michael Arlen arrived, Maugham told me that

Arlen had had just one story to write, and after he had written it three or four times no one would buy it again. At that time he couldn't sell a short story to any editor in America, although he occasionally sold one for a pittance in England. However, Maugham added, Arlen had made a packet when taxes were low and had been shrewd enough to hang onto it.

Occasionally Maugham conveyed his opinion simply by keeping quiet. When Noel Coward was writing one brilliant comedy after another, I remarked that a critic had called Coward a second Maugham. There was a meaningful silence, during which you could have heard a reputation drop. Then Maugham asked me pleasantly if I would like to go for a walk.

Maugham's opinion of a writer, it seems to me, depends in part on which of several categories the writer falls into. He is most generous toward long-dead writers and others with whom he is not in competition—poets, living or dead, non-fiction writers, and small fry. He thinks T. S. Eliot the greatest living poet and heartily agrees with his demand that criticism should be readable. This he would have thought obvious, except that so many critics don't seem to know it. He found Van Wyck Brooks' *Flowering of New England* an enchanting book; he liked Newman White's *Shelley.*

Maugham's lavish praise of Kipling and Dickens is well-known. The latter he qualified by adding that Dickens wrote the English language very badly. From Calcutta he wrote me how delighted he was that he had finally come to India. For years he had resisted going there for several reasons, one of which was a notion that, so far as stories were concerned, Kipling had written all the good ones that were there to be written, and this he discovered to be a fact.

A great many of the literary judgments which Maugham passed in my hearing he incorporated in *Books and You.* There is therefore no point in my repeating them here. I can however report that his published judgments concurred with his private ones.

Novelists who have been his contemporaries, English or American, Maugham is likely to be critical of. He doesn't like *The Magic Mountain;* he said the philosophy Mann made use of is obvious. I don't recall his expressing an opinion of Galsworthy, except as it is implied in his remark that he thought it odd that all aspiring young writers seem to think it necessary to read *The Forsyte Saga.* Bennett he has written about at length, praising the writer and damning the man. He doesn't like Katherine Mansfield's short stories because they break apart in the middle, they have no form. He made the same criticism of Marquand's *Wickford Point,* and he made it years before he may have read in the *New Yorker* profile that Marquand doesn't rate him too highly either. When I asked him what he thought of Thomas Wolfe's novels, he answered, "It's hardly fair to judge him, is it? He died before he mastered his art."

Once I asked him to what extent he thought intelligence was necessary equipment for a novelist. He said it wasn't necessary at all. To be a successful novelist or playwright, one must have a knack of setting forth a dramatic situation, and intelligence has nothing to do with this. "Consider the case of Edna Ferber," he continued. "There's a highly successful novelist."

Henry James is almost an obsession with Maugham. They knew each other when James was an old man, Maugham a relatively young one. On the opening page of *The Razor's Edge* Maugham goes out of his way to take a crack at James; in *Cakes and Ale* he drags him in by having Ashenden recall and repeat a belittling remark which Driffield is supposed to have made: "Poor Henry, he's spending eternity wandering round and round a stately park and the fence is just too high for him to peep over and they're having tea just too far for him to hear what the countess is saying." In *Don Fernando*, a book about the Golden Age of Spanish literature, Maugham digresses to point out that James turned his back on the rise of the United States to a world power in order to exercise his subtlety on the anemic passions of the fashionable world. He doesn't criticize James for this, he says, he merely remarks on it.

In *The Vagrant Mood* there are pages of uncharitable observations, one of them to the effect that James was excessively class-conscious, a criticism which is as applicable to Maugham as it could be to James. Aware that he has made James appear ridiculous, Maugham apologizes for it, but adds that this is the way James struck him. He does not deny James' abilities but thinks they were misdirected. His most serious charge is that James was shy of life and observed it from a safe distance, with the result that his characters are bloodless and unconvincing.

Maugham often referred to James in conversation. He told me all the anecdotes he later included in *The Vagrant Mood*. Shaw was another writer whom he seemed constantly to compare with himself. I don't believe he thinks himself a better writer than James or Shaw, but I think he takes comfort in the fact that he is more versatile. He has been eminently successful as both novelist and dramatist, whereas James in the drama and Shaw in the novel are clearly out of their element.

Maugham's attitude towards younger writers is benign and fatherly. He implies that he has had his day and now it is their turn. Perhaps they have not yet achieved full stature, but when they do, great things are to be expected of them. He knows a number of them personally and takes a special interest in their work. Once Christopher Isherwood came to see him when I was visiting. At that time Isherwood seemed to have given up writing in order to devote himself to the study of Indian philosophy. Maugham remonstrated with him gently. He told him he had a nice talent and it was wrong not to make the most of it. Isherwood assured the Master that he had not really given up writing. Maugham was not damning with faint praise when he used the word "talent." He rates his own abilities no higher.

Noel Coward, John Van Druten, and Tennessee Williams he spoke of in the same rather patronizing way. Though he never compared them with himself, I doubt that he thought they were as good dramatists as he—although I have not heard him express an opinion of any Williams play after *Streetcar Named Desire*. He liked Williams' use of music in it. He didn't care much for *The Glass Menagerie;* he said the last third of it has no structure.

Glenway Wescott's style he thinks precious. Yet Glenway calls Maugham "Master" and is one of the few who have written warmly, if not extravagantly, of Maugham's achievement as a novelist.

I recall his remarks about another group of celebrities, some of whom are writers, whom he spoke of, however, not as writers but as people. Dorothy Parker, in his opinion, is a bitter, unhappy woman, but he admires her sharp wit and its spontaneous, natural quality. She does not, he said, think up a clever remark and store it up for use when she can make the most of it. On a motor trip when there was no one to impress (he evidently didn't consider himself such a one), she was consistently brilliant and witty.

Once *Time* magazine reported an unkind remark which Carl Sandburg made about Maugham. I saw Maugham shortly after and commiserated with him. I wondered why Sandburg had gone out of his way to say what he did.

"Jealousy," said Maugham airily. "Pure jealousy."

One of the few persons Maugham seemed to admire unreservedly was Gandhi. Perhaps he had his reservations, but he never happened to mention them to me. He had an audience with Gandhi when he visited India in 1937. He told me he was led into Gandhi's presence and then a curious thing happened. He fainted. When he was revived he felt weak and sat quietly for a few minutes, saying nothing. Gandhi, presumably to put Maugham at his ease, made a kindly remark which greatly impressed him.

"Silence is also conversation."

THE MAN BEHIND THE MASK

I recall this little anecdote particularly because, some months after he told it to me, Maugham said with obvious irritation that there was a story going around that when he was led into Gandhi's presence he had fainted. Damned silly story, Maugham said.

Maugham's opinion of his friends fluctuates more widely than his opinion of fellow writers. When his friends aren't around, he can be very fond of them, but a little of their society satisfies him. He looks forward so eagerly to their visits that by the time they arrive he has had almost enough of them. He would generously invite you to spend a week with him, but he would be grateful if you found it necessary to leave at the end of five days. New friends give him more pleasure than old ones, for they are unexplored territory. He sincerely admires the pure in heart, but for a steady diet prefers the company of rogues and bridge players.

He has no sentimental attachment to a friend just because he has known him for years. He usually feels that such a relationship has yielded all the pleasure and profit it is capable of yielding, and he despises himself for being too kind-hearted to make a clean break. He once spoke to me of a problem which only the celebrated are faced with. He said that the average person in the course of his life makes and gives up many friends without any ill feeling on either side. College buddies settle in different places and weaken the sacred bonds of fraternity; a close neighbor moves away; business associates change. One feels at first the loss of a friend, but another comes along and the void is filled. But, continued Maugham, no one who snags acquaintance with a celebrated person will ever willingly let him go, and will bitterly resent any cooling off on the other's part. As a consequence, the celebrated acquire an unwieldy and ever-growing herd of friends, most of whom they would gladly shuck off if they could.

He has a technique for getting rid of callers when he wants them to go. When we discussed the problem, I suggested awkward pauses in the conversation as a means of implying that one's welcome was wearing thin. Maugham was horrified. That would be discourteous, he said. His technique is more subtle. When he wants a guest to leave, he rises from his chair, glides toward his guest, extends his hand graciously, and murmurs, "It was really very kind of you to come to see me." This always does the trick. Maugham sometimes forgets that he has let you behind the scenes. When he was in New York the last time, he tried this trick on me. It still worked.

CHAPTER 6

The Money-maker (1931-1939)

MAUGHAM's output during the nine years preceding World War II was incredible, even for Maugham. Between 1931 and 1939, nineteen of his books were published. True, some of these were collections of short stories that had already appeared in magazines, and two were collections of plays. Two were short stories published in book form because no magazine editor would buy them. In the first of these, *The Book Bag*, Maugham is too casual about incest to please the average reader, and in the second, *The Judgment Seat*, God is too casual about adultery. (Both stories appear in later collections.) Two more books were editing jobs, and two were plays. One book, a minor article called *My South Sea Island*, was published by a Chicago bookseller without the author's permission. But however much we whittle down the total, the remainder looks impressive, for it includes three novels, a travel book, and *The Summing Up*.

This prodigious output is the more astounding when we realize that while he was a productive writer, Maugham never devoted more than three hours a day to the job. "If Darwin could work no more than that and change the whole course of human thought," he said, "I saw no reason why I, who never expected to change the course of anything, should work longer." His habit was to awaken early, regardless of the dissipations of the previous evening, and begin the day with a dose of heavy reading—a philosophical treatise or a work by an unreadable writer like Walter Savage Landor. If he didn't feel up to these, he relaxed over a Greek drama. Breakfast was light. After breakfast he got up, and even when the house was full of guests he went to his writing room. If you were wandering around and met him en route, he said no more than a curt "Good morning."

Maugham began his writing chores at eight-thirty or nine. He always wrote with a fountain pen on white, unlined paper. He wrote rapidly and not too legibly, and he wrote in high spirits, for the words came easily. He did not have to scrap draft after draft before getting down something like what he was after. One draft was enough.

This draft, however, was extensively revised, and Maugham said that revision was pleasant, easy work. "The Happy Couple," a short story of twenty-five manuscript pages, shows one hundred and thirty-five alterations of the original text. The original is in blue ink, the revisions in red. A few words he deleted as unnecessary. Often he substituted one word for another. For example, "sprightly chatter" replaced "amusing conversation," and "discomfort" became "malaise." Not infrequently he rewrote a sentence or an entire paragraph. When he did, he drew a line through the rejected material and placed a symbol at the beginning of it. Then, on the reverse side of the preceding page, which was at his left, he repeated the symbol and rewrote the passage. Sometimes he corrected his corrections. "Muttered" became "gasped" and then "cried brokenly." Surprisingly, one revision shows that he changed his mind about a character's appearance. "Thin grey hair" became "thick, strong grey hair."

Maugham could fashion a work of art out of a single draft because writing it down was only the last step in a long process. The daily three hours were not always given over to writing. Sometimes Maugham indulged in what seems like idle reverie. This reverie, he said, was delightful but it was not idle. It was an integral part of the creative process. The basic materials out of which he wrought a short story—a character, theme, or plot—had been in his subconscious mind for months, sometimes for years. The first step in giving birth to the story was to bring this material into his conscious mind. He lived with his characters for weeks. Compared with this life of the imagination, his glittering social life, lived simultaneously, often seemed dull and pallid. In his mind's eye he saw his characters and heard them speak, at first dimly and indistinctly, then clearly. He worked out his plot. Only then did he put pen to paper, and by then the job was largely done.

He wrote without an outline, novels and plays as well as short stories, for he felt that an outline straitjacketed his imagination. Experience taught him that if he gave it a chance, his imagination would suggest incidents which would fall neatly in place and enrich the whole. Before he began *The Razor's Edge*, for example, he knew all of his characters and the general outline of his story, but the idea of Suzanne's exhibition came to him during the writing.

Promptly, at the end of his three-hour stint, the writer bowed out and the gentleman took over. Maugham shuffled his manuscript into a neat pile, for he kept his surroundings as tidy as his mind, and returned to the drawing room. If there were house guests, they now got their courteous due. The makings for drinks appeared, and if he felt like roughing it, Maugham mixed the cocktails himself. His favorite used to be a Gibson, and he concocted a good one. After the right interval, luncheon was announced. It was an elaborate and elegant affair, a series of courses even when he lived in this country during the war and was scrupulous about ration points, but Maugham himself eats rather sparingly. He has a theory that he can keep his health and figure by restricting himself to two courses, and he chooses the two he likes best. When he dines out he will sometimes ask what is coming before deciding whether to make do with what is being offered. He always serves wine, but drinks very little himself.

After lunch he would patiently sip coffee with his guests, but you could see that he craved his nap. He doesn't really like people, his stammer makes talking a strain, and he leaves them with relief. After an hour's rest he awakens and often picks up a detective story. He has read practically every one written, the bad ones as well as the good, and has forgotten them all. Around four he emerges from his room and suggests a walk or a card game.

Then it is time to dress for dinner. Maugham and his guests always dress for dinner, although when he is at home his dress may be unconventional. I recall that one summer he wore a magnificent black Chinese silk outfit, roomy and elaborately embroidered, in which he looked like an elderly chimpanzee in masquerade.

Dinner is preceded by cocktails, and at the Villa Mauresque a footman passes them. They are as cold as we Americans like them; Maugham does not share his compatriates' horror of properly iced drinks. Dinner is more elaborate than lunch, and there is usually champagne. Afterwards there may be cards or just conversation, but not for long; the host is usually in bed by eleven.

This routine isn't inflexible. In New York and London he lives in a hotel and takes most of his meals in his suite, frequently having guests for dinner. When he had completed a novel or other major project, he would give himself a few weeks' rest from writing. In the summer he sometimes varied his writing routine, swimming in the morning when the weather was good and working in the afternoon. He has always carried on an enormous correspondence, and despite the fact that he has a secretary, writes many of the letters himself. He answers all his fan mail; and his fan mail, especially following the publication of a popular novel, was staggering. Even a short piece might touch off an avalanche. A controversial article published during the war called forth three hundred letters, not all of them amiable, and Maugham answered every one of them in longhand.

In addition to business and fan letters, he writes many

to friends. A number of his letters to me begin with an apology for his laziness in taking so long to answer. Lazy he most certainly was not. Only a person of indomitable will would have organized his time and got through his chores as he did.

He is one of those people who like to be burdened with work. Once it occurred to me that I was thoughtless to answer his letters promptly and thereby keep him always in my debt. When I received his next letter I waited a month or so before answering it. He shot back an answer in the next mail. He said he was very glad to hear from me at last, that he couldn't imagine what in God's name had happened to me. After that I answered promptly without compunction.

Sometimes our correspondence languished, and a couple of years might pass before either of us wrote again. I don't believe he ever kept an address book. If he hadn't a letter of mine to answer, he might not remember where to write. Once we so lost track of each other that Maugham, who was coming to this country and thought he might like to see me again, engaged someone to ferret out my hiding place. He told him I had once lived in Washington, D. C. and also had taught in a western college. The detective accomplished his mission by consulting the Washington telephone book.

The critics have long disagreed over Maugham's merits as a writer, but no one questions his genius for making money. Ever since *Lady Frederick* clicked, he has been one of the top money-makers in the business. He has earned more than four million dollars by the sweat of his brow and the power of his pen, much of it before the days of high taxes, and although he has not kept all of it, he has never had to deny himself any luxury, not even philanthropy, and has put aside enough to keep his descendants in caviar and country houses for several generations.

It was not only his incredible output that enabled him to do so, it was also his business sense. He is a shrewd bargainer, not to be softened up by liquor, charm, or obligation to his friend and publisher. In Doubleday's own house the pint-sized Maugham would often back the six-foot Doubleday into a corner. He would begin by remarking with deceptive mildness, "Of course I don't know anything about business, but . . ." and then proceed to show that he knew quite a bit about business, especially as it related to him. Once I accompanied him home after we had dined with the Doubledays and he had exchanged a few friendly words with our host in private. I gathered they had to do with finance, for although he did not favor me with a blow-by-blow account, he remarked with relish, "I told Nelson that his idea of a 50-50 proposition was 75% for him and 25% for me. He didn't like it." It evidently exhilarated him to tell people off.

The artist in Maugham became indifferent to a work the moment he had corrected the proofs, but not the businessman. From Honduras, he peppered his agent with complaints about the unsatisfactory advertising his publisher was giving his books. He demanded enormous advances, not because he needed the money while he struggled to bring forth another masterpiece, but because he was con-

vinced that the only way to persuade a publisher to ad-
vertise a book widely was to force him to invest so much
money in it that he had to invest more to get back his
money.

He demanded top prices for his stories, and he got them.
Several years ago he was offered a contract to make several
phonograph records of his stories. He told me the terms
and asked me to find out how good they were. "Naturally,"
he added, "I am interested in this only for the money."

He could sell his wares in many markets and was not
above playing off one against another. In 1925, when he
was under contract to *Cosmopolitan* for a series of sketches,
he received a letter from London which convinced him
that he was being grossly underpaid, whereupon he wrote
his agent: "I have recently received an offer from *Pearson's*
magazine . . . of two thousand pounds for six stories of
five thousand words each. Of course I refused it but I cannot help knowing that several of the sketches that I have
done for Ray Long [then editor of *Cosmpolitan*] would
have served their purpose very well. I have in point of fact
been making Ray Long in these cases a present of a thousand dollars a story. I am very grateful to him for his
generosity to me and for the admirable advertising he
has given me, but when one's gratitude is costing one a
thousand dollars a month it begins after a while to seem
almost like self-indulgence. I do not know whether you
think it would be worth Ray Long's while to double the
present price of the sketches; if it were, I should be perfectly willing to sign a contract for as many more as he
cared to have. . . . Yours always, Willie."

Maugham's productivity and his talent for selling it at the top of the market did more for his pocketbook than for his reputation. As he himself pointed out, fertility in a writer is a merit only when he is dead. Maugham's fertility during these years gave vogue to the notion that he was little more than a highly competent literary hack, despite the fact that *The Summing Up* and many of the topflight stories were written during these years.

It was not just his fertility that cooled the critics' enthusiasm for his work. It was also the great variation in the quality of the product. During these years Maugham produced as much of his best work as he did in any comparable period of his writing career, but he also turned out much of his worst. It is his contention that a writer should be judged by his best and should be forgiven the potboilers he is obliged to knock out in order to meet the rising costs of maintaining a yacht. In the fullness of time this is what happens, but the uneven writer suffers a different fate during his life. Critics deal severely with him, and they are likely to rate him at his lowest level. They read a *Summing Up* with the recollection of the unkind remarks they made about *Theatre,* published only a year before, and it is not surprising if they do not immediately recognize the superiority of the work at hand.

Throughout his career Maugham's product varied in quality, but it was not always to make a fast buck that he turned out inferior stories. For there came a time when he was more interested in improving his reputation than his bank account. He had achieved his first financial success by writing what he thought the public wanted; now he wrote only what he wanted to write. His income from playwriting had been fabulous, but when playwriting began to bore him, he announced that he was giving it up as soon as he had written several plays he wanted to write, and he ended his dramatic career with *For Services Rendered* and *Sheppey*, two gulps of box office poison that were guaranteed to flop commercially. Rumor has it that he was losing his grip and that he posted his retirement notice because his recent plays had done badly, but the record does not bear this out.

After he passed sixty, however, the thought uppermost in Maugham's mind when he published anything was how it would affect his reputation, not his bank account. He wrote *The Hour Before the Dawn* as a short documentary, and he hesitated a long time before expanding it to novel length. He told me that he didn't care about the money he might make. He didn't want his reputation to fall below whatever it was. He had recently published a novelette. (*Up at the Villa*) and thought it unwise to follow it with another. He did expand *The Hour Before the Dawn*, was dissatisfied with the result, and has never allowed the novel to be published in England.

Although *The Summing Up* has earned him a pretty penny, money-making was certainly not his object in writing it. The numerous books of essays, travel, and criticism were likewise written not for cash but for prestige. There are at least two reasons why the critics continued to call him slick. One is that some of the books he wrote to please himself are no better than those he wrote to please the public. The other is that, having learned how to make money, Maugham seemed unable to write a book that didn't show a tidy profit. Even a substandard work like *Strictly Personal* sold over eighty thousand copies. And since he did not suffer for his high-mindedness, Maugham got little credit for it.

Published in 1932, *The Narrow Corner* is the first product of Maugham's most productive decade. It is in many ways the typical Maugham novel: short, entertaining despite a slender plot, and dominated by persons a little larger than life-size, who always behave in character (which usually means like heels) but sometimes speak out of it. Whatever their temperament, education, or experience, Maugham's chief characters cannot escape grappling with his favorite topics: the meaning of life and the nature of reality.

Maugham did not in his novels follow his recipe for writing a successful play: hew to the story line, and, when you can, cut. If he had, most of his novels would shrink to short-story length, for whereas in the short stories there is usually abundant material which you feel has been compressed, in the novels there is a minimum of story, which Maugham ekes out by making the most of exotic setting, diverting but irrelevant incidents (like the burial at sea in *The Narrow Corner*), and the worldly reflections of a character who dominates the novel but takes no part in the action. Maugham overworks nothing and he keeps things moving, but there is plenty that could be cut without loss to the story. This is why *The Narrow Corner* and several other Maugham novels seem a little thin.

The Narrow Corner has other weaknesses. It is less a novel than a travelogue with a melodramatic ending. Maugham seems to have done here what he considered doing in *Chinese Screen:* woven a connected narrative out of the accumulated notes of a single trip. The result is a novel that breaks in the middle. *The Narrow Corner* is really two long short stories: The first, almost plotless, is the voyage to Kanda-Meira (Banda-Neira in point of fact), which merely introduces three characters; the second is the drama that explodes when they arrive there and their lives are tangled with those of Erik Christessen and Louise Frith. Unlike *The Painted Veil* and *Cakes and Ale,* in which the plot gets going on the very first page, *The Narrow Corner* bobs along pleasantly but pointlessly for half its length; Fred Blake and Louise, whose casual mating leads swiftly to tragedy, do not meet until the novel is half done.

In this novel Maugham rejected the device which chiefly accounts for the effectiveness of *The Painted Veil* and *Cakes and Ale:* projecting his story through the consciousness of a single character. Much of it we get through the eyes of Dr. Saunders, a familiar on-the-side-lines character. But not all. There are scenes in which he is not present, and then Maugham awkwardly shifts the point of view to another character. The result is a weakened impact.

What makes *The Narrow Corner* good reading is Maugham's cast of characters: Fred Blake, whose Greek godliness is balanced by his stupidity and boorishness; the rogue Nichols, who can do a friend dirt yet bear him no malice afterwards; Erik Christessen, the ungainly Dane

whose goodness and sincerity are shattering but a trifle
ridiculous; Frith, the idealist who looks down on practical
people but is not averse to profiting by their industry; and
Frith's daughter, Louise. Louise is the typical Maugham
heroine. She is as serene and self-possessed as a Mother
Superior, but considerably less chaste. She has little book
learning but a wisdom acquired from living. She is dis-
illusioned but not cynical, and although outwardly sub-
missive to the men in her life, she sees through them, is
humorously tolerant of their absurdity, and manages them
effortlessly.

As in many Maugham stories, the most important character in *The Narrow Corner* is one who takes no part in
the action. He is Dr. Saunders, and among the thousands
of characters who people Maugham's novels, short stories,
and plays, it is he who most closely resembles his creator.
Both are inhumanly self-sufficient: they can identify a
quotation you let drop without informing you of the fact,
and enjoy a joke without feeling a desire to impart it to
another. Both are highly diverted by the contrast between
a man's professions and his actions. Neither likes idealists,
who disconcert them by the way they combine their exalted notions with a keen eye for the main chance.

The two gentlemen even look alike: Both are short, ugly
yet elegant, slight but with something of a paunch. When
they laugh, their expressions are "charged with an extreme
but not ill-natured malice." Even in the abandon of
laughter, neither quite gives himself away. If you are not
taken in by their superficial frankness, you sense that
"those laughing eyes are watching, weighing, judging, and

forming an opinion." "It would have been a foolish man who thought they would not see through pretense, but perhaps it would have been a wise one who discerned that . . . they would recognize sincerity. . . . Honesty, however naive, and true feeling, however incongruous," both men "could repay with a sympathy somewhat ironical and amused, but patient and kindly."

Many more passages descriptive of Dr. Saunders are equally applicable to Dr. Maugham. Like Saunders, Maugham "took an interest in his fellows that was not quite scientific and not quite human. He wanted to receive entertainment from them. He regarded them dispassionately and it gave him just the same amusement to unravel the intricacies of the individual as a mathematician might find in the solution of a problem. . . . It was with a little thrill that he sought to pierce into a man's consciousness . . . but the thrill was merely one of curiosity. His sensibility was unaffected. He felt neither sorrow nor pity. . . . He had great natural kindliness, but it was a kindliness of instinct, which betokened no interest in the recipient: he would come to the rescue if you were in a fix, but if there was no getting you out of it would not bother about you further.

"He had fewer prejudices than most men. The sense of disapproval was left out of him. . . . He judged but he did not condemn. . . . Perhaps he was an intensely logical man. . . . He was charitable and kindly . . . but if motive counts for righteousness, then he deserved no praise; for he was influenced in his actions neither by love, pity, nor charity."

The similarity between the men is not only in their temperament and character. The passage in which Dr. Saunders nutshells his philosophy of life reads like a page of the autobiographical *The Summing Up*. "I have never had any sympathy with the ascetic attitude. The wise man combines the pleasures of the senses and the pleasures of the spirit in such a way as to increase the satisfaction he gets from both. The most valuable thing I have learnt from life is to regret nothing. Life is short, nature is hostile, and man is ridiculous; but oddly enough most misfortunes have their compensations, and with a certain humour and a good deal of horse-sense one can make a fairly good job of what is after all a matter of very small consequence."

Yet it would be an error to assume that Saunders is a self-portrait. I have dwelt on the similarities between the two men; there are differences as well. It amused Maugham's sardonic sense to make the character most like himself a bit of a rogue. Moreover, Saunders is not much of a reader; he makes no use of his extensive knowledge of people; he is a better mixer than Maugham, more relaxed and easy-going. He is genuinely indifferent to one's background and table manners. And one pleasure came naturally to him which the fiercely passionate Maugham struggled long to enjoy—the exquisite pleasure of knowing that there was no one in the world who was essential to his peace of mind.

Because he was busy with other kinds of writing, Maugham's next novel did not appear until five years later —1937. In *Theatre* he abandoned his alter ego and projected the story through the consciousness of a woman. She is Julia Lambert, England's leading actress. Unlike Kitty Fane, who wallows in repentance for her sins, Julia takes what she wants from life without regret or apology. She is tough, selfish, aggressive, and amoral. Her love life follows the familiar Maugham pattern: she worships Michael until she marries him, then suffers the pangs of requited love, and achieves a kind of bored contentment only when the exhausting experience is behind her.

All this has happened long before the novel opens; *Theatre* is the story of Julia's affair with Tom Fennell, a boyish bounder years younger than she. The affair gets off to a lighthearted start but it ends badly. Its course, however, is unpredictable. No outraged husband confronts a shamed or defiant wife. Because he is too stupid to see what is going on under his nose, Michael never finds out that his wife has been unfaithful. Nor does Julia suffer through the knowledge that her husband trusts her implicitly, for her conscience is made of sterner stuff. But she does suffer. She becomes extravagantly jealous, first of her son, who becomes great friends with her lover and monopolizes his time; and second of Avice Crichton, a minor actress who supplants her in Tom's bed and affections. Though Julia suffers horribly, the novel has the Maugham version of a happy ending. Avice gets the part she wants but flubs it, and Tom also gets his comeuppance. The emotionally bankrupt Julia feels a wonderful sense of freedom from all earthly ties. Momentarily released from the double bondage of love and diet, she sits down to steak, fried potatoes, and fried onions, crisp and brown.

The house at Parker's, South Carolina

ugham with his daughter,
y John Hope

With his nephew Robin, in South Carolina

Maugham in 1944

Maugham, with the author and Robin

"What is love beside steak and onions?" she asks herself dramatically. "It was an amusing experience."

In this novel Maugham reveals a woman's inmost thoughts and feelings, showing her exactly as she is. It was a daring venture. Julia Lambert being the kind of woman she is, Maugham handed his critics all the ammunition they could wish for. For the charge most frequently leveled against him is that his portraits of women are a libel on the sex. It is true that, like John O'Hara's, his "nice" women—wives and mothers of impeccable background and breeding—are likely to yield suddenly and inexplicably to an impulse to fornicate. This often surprises them as much as it does the startled reader, who when he takes it in feels outraged—not by the immoral act but by its casualness and the speed with which the whole trifling incident is dismissed from their minds. Few persons take kindly to the notion that a hitherto virtuous woman can be seduced in a page and a half and then, the nasty business out of the way, shop for Junior's rompers or hurry home lest Cook forget to rub the lamb with garlic before putting it in the roaster.

Even with the backing of the second Kinsey Report—a book that fascinated him—Maugham will persuade few women readers that he is fair to their sex. Ironically, he himself likes the kind of woman whom his women readers resent—the Louise Friths, the Isabel Maturins, and the Julia Lamberts. He is tolerant of their weaknesses and he admires their candor and honesty.

Ten months after *Theatre*, *The Summing Up* appeared. Maugham had long planned to write a work of non-fiction in which he set forth his views on the subjects that most interested him, but he kept postponing the job because he wasn't quite sure what his views were. When he reached his sixties he decided he had better set himself to the task if he hoped to complete it. He said it would exasperate him to die without writing the book.

Maugham would have us believe that he wrote *The Summing Up* merely to please himself, but the book is surely his most earnest bid for consideration as a serious writer, and his most successful. It eloquently rebuts the charge that he is no more than a teller of tales—a canard for which he is to blame, for he has repeatedly described himself thus.

The Summing Up is difficult to pigeonhole. It is not an autobiography, nor is it a book of recollections. It contains relatively few facts of Maugham's life, and these few relate chiefly to his literary life. It is an honest yet not a warm or chatty book. It is both reticent and embarrassingly frank. Maugham does not mention his marriage, fatherhood, or divorce; yet he casually informs us that, though he has loved and been loved, he has never loved anyone who loved him, and he found it irksome to be the recipient of a passion he could not reciprocate.

Although short, *The Summing Up* is not a book to read in one or two evenings, nor must one necessarily read it consecutively. It is a series of seventy-seven numbered but untitled essays. There is a slight narrative thread which Maugham picks up and drops from time to time, and occasionally an essay begins where the preceding one left off, but each is a self-contained unit and makes excellent reading without reference to what comes before or after.

The essays develop four main topics: Maugham's training as a writer and his analysis of his own character (1–29); playwriting and the nature of the drama (30–42); novel writing, the writing profession, and the psychology of the writer (43–62); Maugham's convictions as to the nature of the universe and how he acquired them (63–77). The first section is the freshest and most personal. The second is the most specialized, for it is an old pro's advice to the aspiring dramatist. Maugham deplores excessive realism on the stage, deprecates the drama of ideas, defends artificial comedy, and otherwise justifies his own practice as a dramatist. Most of this material had already appeared in the prefaces to the collected edition of his plays.

The third section is the most striking. In it Maugham dissects the artist and shows him to be a different animal from other men—more diverse and egotistical, less dependable and sincere. The end of other men is right action, but the end of the artist is production. And he produces not because he wants to but because he must. His spur is the need to liberate his soul of the intolerable burden of creation. Not for nothing, says Maugham, have artists called their works the children of their brains and likened the pains of production to the pains of childbirth. Maugham writes persuasively: the impartial reader cannot but forgive him the popularity and the millions that were the after-birth of this intellectual parturition.

The last section of *The Summing Up* is the least original. In it Maugham says, in his own person, exactly what he said fictionally in *Of Human Bondage.* Since he hasn't changed his views in the twenty-four years between the writing of the two books, one wonders why it was so hard for him to decide what his views were.

Although most readers have found this section the least interesting, it is the most important part of the book for Maugham, for in it he tackles basic questions like Does God exist? (Maybe, maybe not), If God exists, why does he allow evil? (Probably He can't prevent it), Has life any meaning? (No), Is there an after-life? (No). Maugham also weighs the claims of Truth, Beauty, and Goodness to be considered as intrinsic values, and concludes that only Goodness has a valid claim.

Maugham's treatment of these important topics has been called superficial. I suspect that some readers call him superficial because his meaning is always clear. For many intellectuals a measure of obscurity is a necessary ingredient of the profound. In *The Summing Up* there is nothing obscure, nothing awkward. The book exemplifies the stylistic virtues which Maugham extols in it: lucidity, simplicity, and euphony. With the writing of this book Maugham completed the pattern he had set himself to achieve, and with it he reached the acme of his art.

Christmas Holiday followed close on the heels of *The Summing Up.* It is the most controversial of Maugham's novels as to merit. Its admirers consider it the Master's best work: Glenway Wescott calls it the most significant novel published in 1939. In it, he says, Maugham does a masterful job of explaining the nature of Europe's new, self-intoxicated leadership of Fascism and Nazism and Communism, the masses' devotion to the leaders of these *isms* and to the still-to-sprout seeds of evil inherent in them.

Less enthusiastic readers do not deny that something like this is there; the point of difference is whether this socio-economic icing on the cake improves the product or masks its inferior quality. Maugham fans detect a new ingredient in *Christmas Holiday* and most of the novels that follow it. Some of them don't like it. The story's no longer the thing, they say; it's the meaning of the story, its social significance, that counts. Maugham now has a "message" to impart. And some readers feel that Maugham has sold his storytelling birthright for a pot of message.

Of course, in even the slightest pieces of fiction he wrote before this, there is something besides the story; in *Of Human Bondage* Maugham outlined an entire philosophy of life. Readers do not object, because the "message" is implicit in the plot, never obtrusive, and compressed into a few words. They can take it or leave it, and if they choose to leave it, they still have a rattling good story. But *Christmas Holiday* without its social significance is bare bones indeed.

It is an account of Charley Mason's four-day jaunt to Paris, as a result of which, we are told, the bottom fell out of his world. The story is projected through Charley, who is too inexperienced, too unworldly, and too nice a boy to measure up to the exacting role of narrator in Maugham's novels. Where the first-person narrator is wise, calm, and infinitely tolerant of human depravity, poor Charley is stunned by what he sees. There might be a good story in the impact of this frightening new world on the hapless Charley, but he is too well-bred to provide it. He does not plunge into the life suddenly revealed to him. He merely glimpses it through the reminiscences of Lydia, a prostitute who loathes her job but exults in it as a means of atoning for her husband's sin; and through the writings and ravings of Simon Fenimore, an old school chum now grooming himself for a major part in the coming revolution.

There are three separate strands in the novel, and despite his technical virtuosity, Maugham did not succeed in weaving them into whole cloth. As a consequence, *Christmas Holiday* lacks the pace and forward movement of Maugham's best fiction. The first strand, the satire of the pretentiously artistic Masons, was, Maugham told me, bitterly resented in London. It purports to explain Charley by sketching his background in rich detail. It is the most brilliant of the three strands—Maugham at his *Cakes-and-Ale* best—but as a unit of the novel it is disproportionately long, for Charley Mason, though ostensibly the center of the story, is too unimportant a character to deserve the buildup.

The second strand is the story of Charley's four days in Paris. There are vivid scenes, but there is no consecutive narrative and nothing happens, not even the planned adultery which, along with visits to picture galleries, was the purpose of the trip. The third strand, the only one with a plot, is the story of Lydia's married life and her husband's criminal career. Once again we note Maugham's interest in the psychology of the criminal, who, an artist of sorts, steals and murders to fulfill his creative nature.

In March, 1939, Maugham was in this country. Then, as he often did in the spring, he went to London to do some shopping. When he is roughing it in the United States, Maugham will buy himself a suit off the rack at Tripler's in New York, but he always goes to London to buy his underwear because, he says, the British make the best underwear in the world. They have to. The weather, you know.

About the middle of July, he went to the Villa Mauresque, and the summer of 1939 started out like other summers. He expected many house guests, for during the summer he used to do most of his entertaining. His daughter Liza and her then-husband, Vincent Paravicini, were coming, and also his nephew Robin, whose father, Viscount Maugham, was Lord Chancellor of England during the prime ministership of Neville Chamberlain. Robin, who has since followed in his uncle's professional footsteps, although at a respectful distance, was then fresh out of Oxford. Other guests were expected: a duchess or two; a Polish count; David Horner, descendant of Little Jack Horner (whose plum, Maugham said, was an abbey given him by Henry VIII); G. B. Stern; even some Americans. The many bedrooms would always be occupied, and the arrivals and departures of the guests were as carefully worked out as a time table. One guest left on the afternoon Blue train for Paris; before his bed was cold, another had arrived by motor.

Those who came by train got off at Beaulieu, a short distance beyond Nice, and were met by the limousine, Jean, the chauffeur, and Gerald Haxton, the secretary, who escorted them to the Mauresque. It was only a short ride through the fishing village of St. Jean and along the shore of the Mediterranean to the entrance of the estate. The limousine turned in and purred its way up through the terraced garden, past blossoming orange trees and avocado trees and gardeners bent low with reverence and pruning. It stopped before tall green doors, above which one saw the familiar Maugham insignia. Jean assisted one from the car, and at just the right moment Ernest, the butler, flung open the door and ushered one in. There in the hall stood Willie, who greeted one kindly and inquired as to one's health and one's journey. Had one brought maid or valet? If so, quarters were provided for them in some remote part of the house. If not, and one were pigging it on one's own, a maid or valet was provided from Maugham's ample retinue. One's bags were unpacked, one's evening clothes and pajamas laid out. After these had been worn, they were removed and laundered and returned.

Life at the Villa Mauresque before the war was gay and charming and carefree. The ladies, of course, slept late, breakfasted in their rooms, made up their faces at leisure, and put in an appearance about eleven. The men liked to show their stamina by getting up for breakfast and playing a set or two of tennis or swimming several lengths of the pool before noon. When the weather was fine and no luncheon guests were scheduled, the house party often spent a few hours on Maugham's yacht, the *Sara*. They would pile into two or three cars and be driven to Villefranche, where the *Sara* was berthed. If the wind was fair, the *Sara*'s sails carried her out to sea; if not, she was propelled by her auxiliary motor. There she would anchor, so that the party could dive and swim. In the meantime, a member of the crew had whipped up a couple of hearty dishes. These were supplemented by hampers of salad, caviar, *pâté de foie gras*, and wine, which a procession of footmen had packed into one of the cars before leaving the Mauresque. Maugham and his guests then lunched in the simple manner of millionaires on a picnic. Afterwards the host had his nap and the guests napped or read. When the day waned, the *Sara* would steer back to Villefranche, and her passengers would return to the Villa and prepare for the rigors of the evening.

Dinner was served on the terrace overlooking the Mediterranean. Three marble steps led to it from the drawing room, and through the French doors liveried footmen brought course after course in silver dishes. The conversation—sometimes in English, more often in French—was gay and inconsequential, dull perhaps if written down, but thanks to the champagne, the scent of orange blossoms, and the white light of the moon on the marcelled terrace, high-spirited and amusing. Maugham was an excellent host. He sat at the head of the table, speaking little but stage-managing everything. If a guest was silent for long, he would bring him into the conversation. A clever remark addressed to him he would repeat, so that everyone enjoyed it.

It was all as grand and make-believe as one of the host's drawing-room comedies. Everything moved with the seeming effortlessness which plenty of money, thorough organization, and a firm hand at the helm made possible. No guest, when he strolled into the breakfast room, gave Ernest his order, and sat down facing a Laurencin painting, had any notion that two hours before, Willie may have been below stairs pacifying a footman's wife who was accusing a maid of making passes at her husband and threatening to leave—and that on a day when the Windsors were coming to dine.

Entertaining the Windsors was a formidable business. Before the Duke deigned to accept an invitation to dinner, even though it came from a host on his preferred list and he could count on the victuals being good, he had to know who else would be there. And it wasn't just a matter of Willie calling David and asking him and Wally to drop over on Tuesday to meet the So-and-So's. Protocol must be observed; the invitation must be conveyed through channels. Maugham would tell his butler to phone the Duke's butler to inform the Duke that it was just the house party—which might run to a dozen people but all, presumably, adequately screened already—and the Duke would consult his book and then perhaps tell his butler to phone Maugham's butler that they would be pleased to accept.

These occasions were always on the formal side, with a lot of bowing and curtsying and everyone listening intently to what the Duke said, whether it was worth listening to or not. Once the irrepressible Gerald attempted some mild levity. They were playing poker, dealer's choice, and when he was dealer Gerald chose to make all the court cards wild. The Duke was not amused.

On another occasion, the elaborate dinner was followed by several tables of bridge, and during the play the Duchess made a now-famous wisecrack. Maugham was her partner, and as he got the bid, she put down her hand.

"I'm afraid I don't have very much for you, Willie," she said apologetically.

"Oh, I don't know," said Willie, "you have a couple of kings."

"What good are kings?" asked the Duchess dramatically. "They always abdicate."

This story has been printed several times, but no one seems to have caught the sequel to it. Everyone laughed discreetly (the Duke was at another table), and several ladies, with a flutter of their immaculate hands, said they simply must go and wash. They raced each other to the drawing-room door.

"You know," said Maugham, when they were out of the room, "they aren't going to wash their hands. The phone's out there and they want to be the first to report that bon mot along the Côte d'Azur."

Once I asked Maugham whether he thought the Duke of Windsor was intelligent. Maugham considered the question a moment before he answered.

"I don't know about his intelligence," he replied cautiously, "but he's *bien élevé.*"

At this time the Windsor romance was new and glittering. Idealists the world over were fired by that splendid act of renunciation. They lauded the man who couldn't face life without the woman he loved. In the neighborhood of the Villa Mauresque the happy couple were as avid a topic of conversation as they were everywhere else during that summer of 1939, but the theories as to why the King had forsaken his throne for a woman were markedly less romantic than those current on this side of the Atlantic. Some cynics, recalling David's previous attachments, even implied that this one might wear out this side of the grave. Maugham was not one of these cynics. He took the kindly, tolerant view. He said he didn't blame Wally for insisting upon the status of marriage. Of course, had she been British, she would have seen that her duty lay in cheerfully accepting the role of mistress of the king, thereby averting the tragedy of abdication. But why should an American make this sacrifice?

Maugham seldom dined out. He said he was a working man and could not waste time driving forty miles for a meal. Most of his friends, he said, realized his situation and were kind enough to come to him even though he did not return the favor and go to them. Judging by the number of lunch and dinner guests at the Mauresque, I would say that quite a few kind friends were willing to indulge Maugham's eccentricity.

One day when a dozen people were coming to lunch, one of the ladies, an imposing grande-dame type with an especially haughty manner, arrived early. She wasn't very well, Maugham said; in fact, she suffered from what he described as "incontinence of the bowels." Shortly after arriving she felt an attack coming on and, having already found her way around, beat a hasty retreat to a bedroom-and-bath on the first floor. She sped through the bedroom and opened the door to the bath. As it happened, the tub at the moment was occupied by H. G. Wells. However, said Maugham, who described the incident with great relish, "her condition brooked no delay." She entered. Since she utterly ignored him, Wells utterly ignored her. Lying full length in the tub, Wells continued to sponge himself. Neither spoke a word. In due course the lady arose, glanced in the mirror, and swept majestically out of the bathroom. Ten minutes later she and Wells were formally introduced in the drawing room and neither batted an eye.

July turned into August, and black clouds loomed above. The possibility of war was vaguely referred to at times, but such talk was considered ill-bred. It was proper to mention war only if you could give a reason why there wasn't going to be one. Someone remarked that of course there couldn't be a war because Hore-Belisha—then British Secretary of State for War—was on the Continent, and if there was going to be a war, he would obviously be in England. Maugham said he hoped Hitler realized that.

Below stairs there was muttering. Without warning, Italian footmen left to go back to Italy to join up; but the ranks of the deserters were promptly filled by the firm in Nice which supplied the Mauresque with manpower and sent an agent out once a week to pay the staff. In the spacious rooms of the Mauresque the war clouds were mostly ignored. There were more immediate worries. One day the household was thrown into an uproar because Erda,

Maugham's favorite dachshund, gave every sign of being pregnant, and the father was certainly itinerant and unpedigreed. Maugham's tolerance of erratic human behavior did not extend to dogs; he was very upset.

On another occasion the unsanctified behavior of humans created the problem. A maiden lady, an old friend, was coming for a visit. Though she was sixty-five, she had a mother still living. Through some miscalculation in the timetable she had been invited for a time when the house party included a lady and gentleman living in sin. Out of delicacy Maugham wrote her and explained the situation, adding that he hoped it wouldn't make any difference in her plans. Her answer postponed the visit. She was, she wrote, perfectly broadminded about such things, "but Mother wouldn't approve."

These upsets Maugham took in his stride, and life at the Villa Mauresque went on its carefree way. "Anyone for tennis?" was still the cheerful cry in the morning, and at noon the *Sara* sailed out with her cargo of caviar and blue blood, and sailed back when the sun was over the yardarm. Guests continued to arrive and depart on schedule, but there were fewer of them. August drew to a close and the rich looked ahead to the fall season. Some faced up to the fact that a sojourn at a spa for their health's sake was indicated, and bravely took their leave. The Blue train was booked solid. Maugham made his plans to go to India again for the winter, where he was gathering material for his new novel. In the meantime the days were still lovely, the sea was calm and blue, and there was plenty of good bridge. One lived in the halcyon present.

CHAPTER 7

The War and Willie (1940-1946)

THEN suddenly it happened. The mayor of St. Jean phoned and respectfully informed the Master of the Mauresque that the order of mobilization would be posted the following day. That night another Italian servant disappeared from the villa, and in the morning the chauffeur told Maugham that his class had been called up and he would have to rejoin his regiment. Black Senegalese troops mysteriously appeared on the roads, guarding the bridges. Maugham's daughter and son-in-law and the remaining guests hurriedly departed.

The harbormaster at Villefranche notified Gerald Haxton that an order had come through from the naval base at Toulon that all private yachts must leave within twenty-four hours. After a hurried conference, Willie and Gerald decided to sail the *Sara* to Cassis, where there are a number of secluded creeks. As they were about to leave the Mauresque, a young English couple appeared. In the excitement of the morning Maugham had forgotten that he had invited them and they, having a lovely holiday in the south of France, had gaily overlooked the grim signs of war. They thought the Senegalese troops were very picturesque. Maugham convinced them they had better start driving back toward England while they still had a car to drive and could buy gas, and they departed reluctantly. Willie and Gerald made for the shops in Nice to buy provisions for the *Sara*, but many people had got there first and they had to content themselves with odd cans of this and that.

Though it was a fine day when the *Sara* sailed out of the harbor, Maugham was filled with rage. A force greater than himself had gashed the carefully wrought pattern of his life. But Maugham can always rise above major emergencies. He shouted the dirtiest words he knew—unfortunately, no one thought to record them for posterity—and then he put on his bathing trunks and lay in the sun. Soon he was resigned, and then content. Besides, he knew the French army was invincible. It was a nuisance being driven away from one's home and garden, but in a few weeks all would be over and he would be back. His chief concern was that the French might requisition his villa and quarter troops there. He knew that the military are apt to be childishly destructive, and he did not fancy having them test their markmanship by firing at his pictures. As he could do nothing about it, he soon put the matter out of his mind. The *Sara* anchored and he went overboard for a swim. Then they proceeded to Ste. Maxime, where he had friends who he thought could be counted on to provide a good dinner, war notwithstanding.

At dawn the next day they set out again. Because the

waters near the coast were mined, they had to go out to sea, and a heavy storm blew up which got worse as the day wore on. At night they were forced to steer by compass because the lights on the shore had been extinguished. The next day, the storm still raging, they took refuge in a quiet cove and sat it out. Two days later they resumed their journey. The sea was still choppy and they had another worry. They had to pass Toulon, and if war was declared before they got by, they might be turned back. When they came in sight of the naval base they saw a small boat making for them. They watched it nervously. Would they be allowed to pass? Thanks to Maugham's foresight, they were. Several years before, when he had bought the *Sara,* Maugham considered the possibility of war. The *Sara* was registered in the name of Gerald Haxton, an American, and the Stars and Stripes flying from her stern protected them. The small boat turned back, and the *Sara* proceeded on her way.

By this time Maugham had had a bellyful of yachting. He says you need a peculiar temperament to enjoy being tossed about hour after hour in a small boat, and he doesn't have it. A yacht is something you acquire when your income reaches a certain point. It is a mark of prestige, not a mode of transportation. They decided to make for Bandol rather than Cassis, for according to the *Mediterranean Pilot,* Bandol has a good harbor. Two hours later they entered it, found a vacant berth, and tied up.

Maugham had never been to Bandol, for although a seaside resort, it is not a fashionable one. With Gerald and the crew of three, he settled down to a quiet life. Each day

he went ashore, got a shave at the barber's and a loaf of
bread at the baker's, drank his *café au lait* and read the
paper. Then he did the marketing. Everyone had to work,
and the gourmet Maugham seemed the logical choice to
select the victuals. As it turned out, the cabin boy could
have done better, for never before in his sheltered life had
Maugham encountered food in its raw naked state. The
honest French marketwomen, recognizing an innocent,
took full advantage of him, and they dined on tough
chicken, unripe cheese, and rotten melon.

When they had been in Bandol about a week, the news
came through that the Germans had marched into Poland
and war was declared. All able-bodied men left the town,
and the casino was turned into a hospital. Things gradually
got worse. Two of the three-man crew departed, and the
Sara's portholes had to be blacked out. They had to give
up the charming custom of dining on deck and crowd
themselves into the hot cabin. Maugham added sweeping
and tidying up to his other household chores.

The days dragged by. Some weeks before, Maugham
had put out feelers for war work should war be declared.
Now, chafing at his inaction, he decided to leave the *Sara*
in Bandol and go back to the Mauresque, where he hoped
to hear from the British Ministry of Information, to whom
he had addressed his offer. Getting back to the Mauresque
presented a problem. Since the declaration of war, people
were not free to move about as they pleased, and foreigners
were forbidden to move from one department to another
without express authorization. Before they could officially
leave Bandol and pass through the military zone of Toulon,

they had to get papers which it would take weeks to wangle. Police examined these papers before one was allowed on a train and when one got off. The situation looked hopeless.

But Maugham, who has extricated his characters from many a tight situation, figured a way out of this one. He simply hailed a taxi, got in, and said to the astonished driver, "Cap Ferrat." They drove out of Bandol, into and out of security-conscious Toulon, with no one paying the slightest attention to them, and that night they were home in the Villa Mauresque, where Erda, the favorite dachshund, gave her master a tumultuous welcome. Among Maugham's letters was an answer from the Ministry of Information accepting his offer to do anything they wanted him to do and informing him that he should hold himself in readiness for another letter, which would follow. It did, weeks later. Maugham had hoped he wouldn't be asked to write, he thought that his spying experience in the First World War would fit him for some such activity in this one; but when the letter came he learned that he was to write a series of articles about France in wartime and the French war effort. He was also to find out what he could about the attitude of the French towards their British allies.

Maugham thereupon journeyed to Paris, where arrangements were made for him to visit the places where he could get his material: the munitions factories, the naval base at Toulon, the front, and the areas where those who had been living near the front had been resettled. Maugham wrote me that the job he had been asked to do was small and unimportant but, he hoped, useful. He went where he was asked to go, saw a great deal, and put some of it in a series of articles which in 1940 were bound into a paperback and entitled *France at War*.

Nothing Maugham published during his maturity embarrassed him so much as *France at War*. It was journalism and he was not, he admitted, a good journalist. Because the book was intended as propaganda, he was obliged to omit a good many distressing facts he had observed and to put the best possible face on those he included. Although he was disturbed by the lukewarmness of the French war effort and distressed by the antagonism which the French freely expressed for their British allies, Maugham wrote, "I do not believe that we in England yet realize how intense the French effort is." On the title page of my copy of *France at War* Maugham wrote, "The result, the inaccurate result as events showed, of a tour made for the British government in the autumn of 1939." One motive for writing *Strictly Personal* (his next book, and also substandard) was to tell the truth which, before the fall of France, he didn't dare tell.

France at War having been completed, Maugham was told to come to England, where other work awaited him. In *Strictly Personal* he describes England as he found her at this time and bitterly attacks his countrymen for their casual attitude toward the war. The restaurants and the theatres were crowded, and when he lunched at the Ritz he saw everyone he knew. They had to eat somewhere, they said, so why not at the Ritz? He went to a dinner party where there were three cabinet ministers, and after the ladies had left them the gentlemen sat long over their port and discussed the advantages of an old-fashioned classical education.

The stinging rebukes implicit in these social notes have an odd sound on Maugham's lips. They imply that while Rome burned, only he didn't join in the fiddling. One could as fairly criticize Roosevelt for devoting the odd hour to his stamp collection while the outcome of the war was still in doubt. Lunching at the Ritz is not proof of irresponsibility, nor is a sandwich at the desk an infallible mark of a faithful public servant. Rather than attack his countrymen, one would expect Maugham to defend them against just such a charge as he is guilty of. The frightful experiences he had recently undergone had temporarily dislocated his sense of proportion. He is not detached and urbane; he is seething with moral indignation.

One explanation, of course, is that this was written during the heat of war, before the tide had turned in the Allies' favor. Maugham found in the United States the same apathy that shocked him in England, and he hoped to urge us out of it. There is, however, a less obvious explanation. For some time Maugham had been shucking off his youthful flippancy as unbecoming his increasing age. The new Maugham is a basically serious man, much concerned with moral values. His sense of humor is less light-hearted. He would never again write an *Our Betters*, in which he glamorized the morally corrupt Pearl Grayston. The new Maugham wrote *Sheppey*, in which the hero tries to live like Jesus and for his pains barely escapes being committed to an insane asylum by his wife and daughter. The war did not effect the metamorphosis of Maugham—*Sheppey* was written in 1933—but it speeded up the process.

Maugham spent three months in England trying in vain to find something useful to do. He said he was like a performing dog whose tricks the public would probably like, but who somehow couldn't be fitted into the program. Then he was shipped back to France to write more articles for an illustrated paper and to do a little part-time spying on Britain's ally. Less than a week after he arrived in Paris, the Germans invaded Belgium and Holland, and the new scheme came to nothing. Maugham returned to the Villa Mauresque.

His faith in the invincibleness of the French army was still unimpaired. As evidence of it, he ordered 20,000 tulip bulbs to be delivered for planting in September. The capitulation of the Belgian army, the British retreat to the sea and escape from Dunkirk were staggering blows, but did not destroy his confidence. Then he learned that Paris was not to be defended and the government had fled to Bordeaux. The final blow came when Pétain was made head of the government and announced over the radio that France must sue for peace.

Maugham then realized his personal danger. The Mauresque is only a few miles from the Italian border, and the Italians might come at any moment. Moreover, Goebbels had denounced *Ashenden,* his book based on his experiences as a spy in the First World War, and Maugham had reason to think that he was marked for special handling. He hastened to Nice, where he learned from the

British consul that two coal ships had been requisitioned to transport British subjects to England. He was told to be at the quay in Cannes at eight the next morning, bringing with him a handbag, a blanket, and three days' provisions. Maugham returned to the Mauresque, where he took a last look at his garden, his pictures, and the room where he had hoped to die. He considered dying then and there, but finally decided to take his chances. Into the one bag he was allowed to bring he put sugar, tea, macaroni, marmalade, and bread; but no can opener, plate, knife, or fork. He looked longingly at a beautiful new tail coat but, sensibly concluding that he might never again have occasion to dress formally, packed his dinner jacket instead.

The voyage to England took twenty days and was incredibly uncomfortable, dirty, and dangerous. The 4000-ton vessel was packed with refugees, many of them old, all of them frightened. Several died en route, and four went mad. The world press reported that Maugham had disappeared and was probably dead.

This time Maugham remained in England several months. When there appeared to be nothing he could do, he decided to come to the United States, and after some weeks of negotiations he was allowed to do so. With ten pounds in his pocket—all he was allowed to take out—he flew to Lisbon, and after a week's delay got a place on the New York clipper. He had never flown such a distance before and expected to be frightened, but he wasn't except when they ran into a storm and the plane bumped alarmingly. Since he couldn't get out and walk, he wisely decided to take a sleeping pill and relax. He said it was fun having dinner in the Azores and breakfast in Bermuda. At New York's LaGuardia Airport, he spent the last of his ten pounds on a Martini. It was October 1940.

Although he had plenty of money stashed here and there, Maugham was in something of a jam. Still, his situation wasn't as serious as that of most refugees, and his standard of living did not suffer any real decline. He stayed at the Ritz as usual, where his suite was dark but comfortable. He kept cheerful. If God wouldn't provide, plenty of editors would. He was immediately besieged with offers. *Collier's* wanted him to write a book about his experiences since the beginning of the war, and he thought it might be fun to do so. He was soon as busy as ever, and the money began rolling in again.

There was a catch, however. The money didn't roll into his pocket. When he left England, Maugham agreed to live on $1500 a month, only a fraction of his income. The remainder was impounded in England for the duration. He could have got all he wanted from his American publisher, but he said he considered it a contribution to the war effort to struggle along on the pitiful sum allowed him. When I hinted that I could make do on $1500 a month without inconvenience, he made a sensible answer.

"Of course you could. You're a college professor and everybody knows you haven't a cent. But I am supposed to have money, and I have obligations."

One of these was his daughter Liza, who, with her mother and her two children, was also living in New York. Father gave daughter $300 a month, and it irked him that his ex-wife, whose brief services he had amply recompensed at the time of the divorce, shared Liza's bounty.

Maugham had planned to leave the Ritz and settle down in a New York apartment, but Hollywood crooked a golden finger. Maugham and his secretary went west. Gerald had remained in France after Willie left, hoping to salvage some of the art treasures in the Mauresque. Then he flew to Lisbon and eventually to New York.

During the war years Maugham spent considerable time in the movie colony, short periods in a hotel, longer periods in a rented house. He always professed to dislike the place, but he seems to have spent more time there than he needed to perform his movie chores. People were cordial and hospitable, he said, and he supposed he could go to a party every night if he wanted to. But he could find no one who was willing to talk of the things he was interested in; it was like having nothing to eat but candy.

Once when I was staying with him in a house he had rented in Beverly Hills, an incident occurred which showed how he felt about some of the movie people. Liza was also visiting him at the time, and one evening she was being squired by one of the more glamorous of the stars. Maugham and I were in the library having a gimlet before our dinner. The butler announced the movie star. I could see that Maugham was vexed, he had expected the man to be ushered into the drawing room to await Liza, but he offered a drink and tried to make conversation. The evening paper had contained some heartening war news, all too rare at that time, and Maugham asked eagerly, "Did you see the news?"

"You mean about Mickey Rooney?" the star responded. Maugham switched topics but the swashbuckling hero of many a stirring screen epic could cope with none of them. He seemed as tongue-tied as his stammering host. After what seemed like an hour—and was probably no more than ten minutes—Liza appeared, a few pleasant remarks were exchanged, and the two of them departed. As soon as they were out of earshot Maugham said irritably, "I've told Liza I don't care what kind of people she knows provided I don't have to meet them."

While he was in Hollywood, Maugham used his pen to make another contribution to the war effort. As a Britisher living in the United States during the war, he early became conscious of the bad feeling not far below the surface friendliness that Americans expressed for their British allies, and he wanted to bring about a genuine friendliness. Facing the issue boldly, he wrote an article called "Why D'You Dislike Us?" It appeared in the *Saturday Evening Post* and was widely read. The initial response was not encouraging. A great many people obliged him with letters in which they answered his question at length. But the tone of the article is tactful and conciliatory, and it no doubt effected much good among unprejudiced readers. Maugham planned another article with the same lofty aim. He set himself to study the British and American accounts of the Revolutionary War and the War of 1812, hoping to write something that would reconcile them. But, although he went back to New York to provide himself with adequate library facilities, the project was too ambitious for an amateur historian and he eventually abandoned it.

Another contribution to the war effort Maugham completed, but he was deeply dissatisfied with it. *The Hour Before the Dawn,* the poorest novel of his maturity, was written at the request of the Ministry of Information and was intended to show the effect of the war on a typically British family. Maugham told me that several times while writing it he would have chucked it except that he considered it his duty to finish it. He didn't care enough about it to give it a title, which was supplied by his publisher. The novel failed because it was written to order. Maugham simply couldn't write good fiction that way. It was published in 1942, and in 1944 was made into a successful movie starring Veronica Lake and Franchot Tone.

At the beginning of December, 1941, Maugham moved from New York to what was to be his American home for the duration of the war. The house was called Parker's and was built for him by Nelson Doubleday on his plantation twelve miles from Yemassee, South Carolina. About a mile from Bonny Hall, the big plantation house, Parker's is an eight-room English cottage with a river at its front door. Maugham did not see it until it was completed. He had stipulated that he wouldn't live in it if he didn't like it.

Parker's wasn't ready for him when he arrived, nor for some time after, for, like everybody else at that time, Maugham had difficulty getting the right materials and the people to do the necessary work. The plumber and the electrician (one and the same person) hadn't put in the furnace or got the lights to work because the plumber was often drunk and the electrician was standing for Congress. There were no shrubs outside the house, and only half the furniture had arrived from Macy's.

When everything was at last in order, Maugham was very pleased. The house, he wrote, was comfortable and the countryside wild, lonely, monotonous, and lovely. The Doubledays lent him a horse and a young Negro to accompany him on his rides and see that he came to no harm. A few weeks later Maugham journeyed back to New York to spend his sixty-eighth birthday with the Doubledays. They gave him a cake and lots of presents and he felt he had fared very well indeed. People never made a fuss like that over him in England, he said.

Parker's was simple living after the luxury of the Mauresque, but Maugham wasn't exactly roughing it. The house had three bedrooms, each with its bath, a small sitting room which no one ever sat in, a bright dining room, a large cheerful living room, an entrance hall, and a kitchen. On the walls were reproductions of paintings that Maugham had had to leave behind in the Mauresque.

He was taken care of by a cook, Nora, and Mary, whom he described as a parlor maid. When I first saw Nora and Mary, they were slim and straight. Before Maugham left South Carolina permanently, they were fat. Maugham said this was because he insisted that the servants eat the same food he ate. They evidently ate a great deal more of it than he did.

When I have visited Maugham in homes and hotels in which he lived in various parts of the world, I have noticed that his servants are invariably devoted to him. The chambermaid in the hotel where he spent his summers darned his socks in addition to performing her regular duties although, she told me, Maugham was an adequate but not a lavish tipper. Servants liked him because he invariably treated them with consideration. He might be rude to a friend, but never to a servant. Once when I was staying with him in Beverly Hills I happened to come in about five in the morning, and to my astonishment I met the butler, who lived out, arriving at the same time. I asked him why he came to work at such an hour and he said he liked to have everything nice for Mr. Maugham.

In addition to Nora and Mary, Parker's had a yardman named Sunday. Sunday wore dark glasses indoors as well as out because he thought they made him look chic. His nephew Religious—the name delighted Maugham—did occasional odd jobs around the place. It was a far cry from the Villa Mauresque with its staff of thirteen catering to the comfort of one old party, but it was cozy living just the same. Despite rationing, Nora turned out some tasty meals. When Maugham engaged her, she was already a good southern cook and Maugham, who knows all about food but can't make a cup of tea, taught her to prepare French dishes. Maugham's taste in food is as cosmopolitan as his taste in literature; he is fond, for example, of Boston baked beans. Nora was an apt and willing pupil, but she drew the line at preparing Yankee food, and Maugham had to wait until he went north to get his baked beans.

Maugham spent the winters of 1941 to 1946 at Parker's.

His life there was much quieter than he had been accustomed to. It was too quiet for Gerald Haxton, who took a war job in Washington. Occasionally a friend spent a few days with him, but most of the time Maugham was alone. His days followed pretty much the same pattern. Mary brought him his breakfast at eight: stewed fruit, coffee, toast, sometimes an egg. On Sunday there were pancakes. After breakfast Maugham did his heavy reading, often philosophy. He was especially interested in oriental mysticism, and he put his knowledge of it to good use in *The Razor's Edge*. The rationalist Maugham seems always to have been fascinated by what the rational mind rejects. At nine he left the house and walked to his writing room, where he remained until noon.

The writing room at Parker's was a one-room bungalow a few yards from the main house. It was always neat and tidy. There was a fireplace, and on the floor was a white rug. On the desk, neatly arranged, was the manuscript Maugham was working on at the time.

When Maugham was working you didn't disturb him, and you saw to it that others didn't. I recall an incident when an uninvited visitor was determined to see him and I, with some trepidation, prevented him from doing so. It was February, 1943. In the course of the morning Mary came to my room and told me that two gentlemen had asked to see the Master. I went into the living room and greeted a Marine colonel and a general. The colonel said he was a good friend of Willie's and would like to introduce him to the general. I explained that Willie was working and wouldn't like to be disturbed, though of course he would be distressed to miss them. The colonel repeated patiently that he was a very close friend and he was sure it would be all right.

I was in a quandary. High-ranking officers were godlike beings in those days. About to put on a uniform myself, I was properly awed. But I knew that the hours from nine to twelve were sacrosanct. I asked the gentlemen if they wouldn't please wait until noon. The colonel answered curtly that of course they couldn't. The air was electric with ill will. Finally they got up and stomped out of the house. I followed humbly. Suddenly the colonel, stepping nimbly in the direction of the writing room, said he guessed he'd just look in for a minute. I leaped in front of him, barring the way.

"Oh no you won't, Colonel."

The colonel glared, I trembled, and the air quivered. Inside the writing room all was quiet, though Willie must have heard something of what was going on. Then, without another word, the two officers got into their car and were driven off.

I had won that round, but I wasn't happy. What if the colonel were really a good friend? Had I exceeded my authority? I now realized that I had acted, not solely to protect Maugham's privacy, but in some obscure way to take the enlisted men's part against his natural enemy. What would Willie say? I imagined him asking me crossly why the devil I hadn't minded my own damned business. Time dragged but eventually it was twelve and the methodical Maugham put down his pen and sauntered over to the house. I waited until we had drunk our gimlet before describing the morning's skirmish.

"Should I have let them see you, Willie?"

"Good Lord no," said Willie.

One of our diversions at Parker's was reading the daily quota of fan mail. The number of letters in a given mail depended on how recently Maugham had published a book or article and how much interest it had stirred up, but every mail brought some. A popular novel like *The Razor's Edge* elicited hundreds of letters extending over many months.

There were occasional nut letters, but most letters were pleasant. Most fans thanked Maugham for the pleasure he had given them and hoped for nothing but a reply. Some letters came from young writers who wanted to know Maugham's "formula." The most unusual fan was an eleven-year-old girl who sent the Master a picture she had drawn for him. The Master kept it on his bedside table for some weeks. Another atypical fan was a concert pianist who used to say thanks by playing for Maugham when he was in New York. A few letter writers seemed to look upon Maugham as a man of incredible wealth anxiously searching for a cause to support, and they stood ready to assist him. They asked him to buy them libraries or pay for operations they needed.

During the war many letters came from servicemen, and Maugham seemed particularly pleased by these. Occasionally they would send checks, asking him to send them copies of his books that they hadn't been able to get, and Maugham would send the books and destroy the checks. One letter began, "I want you to know the sheer enjoyment I have derived from your work. It did much to fill in many lonely hours for this marine." It ended, "Respectfully yours." A navy lieutenant asked Maugham to recommend books for him to read. Men overseas often requested that a reply be sent on regular stationery rather than V-mail, which would arrive as a photograph of the coveted original.

Some letters were unconventional, like the one that started, "This may find you in a mellow mood, but I doubt it." Another asked Maugham to send the writer sleeping pills so that she could commit suicide.

The fan letters were a mixed blessing. They cheered the ego but they had to be answered. Maugham answered them all in longhand and did all he could to help those who asked for help. But like all persons in the public eye he has to guard against the maneuvers of people who seek to attach themselves to him for their own profit. One technique occasionally employed to get acquainted is to send a bottle of champagne to his table when he is dining in public. I recall an incident of this sort that had an unexpected outcome.

We were having dinner in the Oak Room of the Plaza in New York. A waiter come to the table with the usual bottle and the usual note that it had been sent by an admirer of Maugham's writing. Maugham sighed. People were so damned kind, he said. He supposed he would have to ask them over. Then, to the waiter, "Ask them if they would care to join us."

"But Mr. Maugham," the waiter answered, "they have already left the room."

Maugham almost flipped. He was so touched by this gesture that he went to considerable trouble to find out who the people were and write them.

When people recognize him in public and speak to him, he is painfully embarrassed, but he has schooled himself to answer civilly. Once in the lobby of a theatre I saw people nudge each other and point to him, and I told him he had been recognized. He said, "That shows that the photographs aren't too bad." He had a notion, most unusual among people in the public eye, that a man's photographs should look like him.

Maugham at this time was writing *The Razor's Edge*. He had given up trying to further the Allied cause with his pen, for despite his dedication to the job the best he could contribute was two bad books. After several years of devoted effort, he came to the painful conclusion that an over-age writer was perhaps wise to ignore the troubled world around him and stick to what he knew best.

The germ of *The Razor's Edge* was a chance meeting at a dinner party in Chicago in 1919, just as Maugham states in the first chapter. The prototype of Larry Darrell was not, as literary gossip had it at the time, Maugham's friend Christopher Isherwood, although Isherwood, like Larry, is much interested in oriental philosophy. Larry's prototype was a young man at the dinner party, and Maugham never saw him again. He remembered just one remark the young man made, to the effect that he didn't want to go into the family business and hoped instead to make something interesting of his life.

The novel has a long history. In 1924, Maugham wrote a play called "The Road Uphill," which is an early version of the novel. It never came to anything, he said, and it was neither produced nor published. That is fortunate, for as a play it would almost certainly have flopped and Maugham would have wasted material he made good use of years later. Five characters of the novel—Larry, Isabel, Gray, Brabazon, and Elliott Templeton—appear in the play under different names, and the plots of the two works are similar. There are differences, of course. There is no mysticism in "The Road Uphill," nor does Larry journey to India. As a matter of fact, there is not as much India in the novel as Maugham wanted. He had gone there in 1937 and had planned to go again in the fall of 1939. Since he wasn't able to, he reduced the role of India in the novel. The reader is never actually transported there; he gets India second-hand through Larry's account of it to the narrator.

"The Road Uphill" also contains the germ of "The Alien Corn," one of Maugham's finest short stories. This story was returned to the dramatic form when it became one of the units which make up the movie *Quartet*.

Unless I asked him, Maugham rarely made any reference in my presence to what he was working on, but I recall one occasion at Parker's when he came into lunch practically purring. He volunteered the information that he rather liked the scene he had just written. He described it in enough detail so that I later recognized it as the bitchy exchange between Elliott Templeton and Marie de Florimond in the third section of Chapter 2 of *The Razor's Edge*.

I can date the writing of this novel quite accurately because I happen to have letters from Maugham telling me that he was about to begin it, that he had finished the first draft, and that he had completed the revision. He began the novel about the middle of November, 1942, at Parker's; on May 12, 1943 he had completed it and was taking it north with him. He planned to take a few weeks' rest and then to revise it. He expected to have it polished up by the middle of August. As a matter of fact, he completed it ahead of schedule. On July 14 he wrote from Edgartown, Massachusetts, that it was done and that he had mailed me the first five chapters and the others would follow as soon as they had been typed.

I saw a number of Maugham's stories in manuscript or typescript before publication, but this is the only one he sent me, and the reason was that I was supposed to go through it and point out any remarks of his American characters that didn't sound like bona fide American language. He said he didn't expect to make them sound absolutely genuine, that was impossible, but he didn't want them to say anything too startlingly British. With characteristic modesty he added that he would be delighted if I pointed out any other flaws I found. He said he might not agree with me, that he hadn't agreed with Desmond McCarthy's objection to the ending of *The Narrow Corner*, but that he couldn't possibly be offended by any criticism. Unfortunately, I wasn't able to oblige; the typescript followed me from Hawaii to Australia to New Guinea but never caught up with me.

Maugham was glad to have done with *The Razor's Edge*. He said he didn't care whether people liked it or not, he had got it off his chest and that was all that mattered to him. He was kidding himself. The critics had panned his recent offerings, and I think he steeled himself against the same kind of reception for this book. He wouldn't read the reviews, but when I visited him some months after the novel had appeared and told him that it had been widely and favorably reviewed, he was obviously delighted.

The Razor's Edge contains some of Maugham's best writing. Elliott Templeton's death scene is shattering, and the last pages of the novel (in which, among other things, he pays his respects to us Americans) are Maugham at his most subtly ironic. The cast of characters is perhaps the most brilliant he ever assembled. Yet the novel marks his decline as a novelist, for in order to show he is more than a storyteller, Maugham stirs in great gobs of religious mysticism, which threaten to smother the narrative. Realizing that this material is irrelevant, he packed it into one long chapter and tells the reader at the beginning that he can skip it if he likes.

There is another reason why *The Razor's Edge* shows a falling off—Maugham's age. He was sixty-nine when he finished it. He could still write brilliant scenes, but he could not tie them all together into a neat, coherent whole. His powers of invention, never his strongest point, failed him and the plot lacks movement and surprise. The novel is put together according to the same tired pattern: a narrator (named Maugham) encounters a group of people at intervals over a period of years and gives us their story.

Yet, thanks to its characters, the novel has life and vitality. The saintly Larry Darrell was supposed to dominate it, but the sinner Elliott Templeton took over. Though no two men are more different on the surface, Maugham and Elliott have something in common, for Maugham has endowed Elliott with many of his own worst qualities, plus a few of his best. Elliott is Maugham if Maugham had let the frivolous side of his nature have the upper hand. A converted Catholic, Elliott is snobbish, vain, finicky, kindly, and generous. He imagines himself descended from the Spanish Count de Lauria, a nobleman of Philip II's court, and instructs his survivors to bury him in a costume such as the Count might have worn. His dying words, "The old bitch," describe an old friend, a hostess who had failed to invite him to a grand party.

Hollywood bought *The Razor's Edge* for $250,000 and paid out another $3,000,000 to make a movie of it. Maugham spent the summer of 1945 in Hollywood working on the script. He stayed with his friend George Cukor because he thought the job they had asked him to do would take no more than a couple of weeks. It took three months. Cukor, Maugham said with astonishment, remained as delightful a host as he had been in the beginning. In his place, Maugham said, he would have made it quite clear to a guest that he had outstayed his welcome.

Maugham liked script writing. It was new work for

him, and he said he found it easy and interesting; he thought the studio was pleased with what he had done. Be that as it may, in the picture Maugham's name is not included as script writer. Lamar Trotti took over where Maugham left off, and wrote twelve versions before coming up with something that satisfied all hands. The studio was just about to start shooting when the end of the war made it possible to get someone better to play Larry, so the picture was shelved for a while. Maugham said that the unfortunate youth whom they had trained for the part was plunged into despair. When *The Razor's Edge* was finally made, Tyrone Power, in his first role after three years as a Marine aviator, played the ex-aviator Larry; Gene Tierney was Isabel; Clifton Webb was a natural for Elliott; and Herbert Marshall impersonated Mr. Maugham.

Maugham spent the summers in Edgartown on Martha's Vineyard. Before he decided to go there, he investigated summer resorts with his usual thoroughness. Because of gas rationing he had to find a place where he could swim near the hotel, and he wanted sailing, bridge, comfort, and quiet. Edgartown seemed to fill the bill, for he returned there each summer he remained in this country.

Maugham's arrival on Martha's Vineyard in July, 1942, was without fanfare. The island is accustomed to celebrities. In fact, the Edgartown Yacht Club phoned the local newspaper—the famous *Vineyard Gazette*—and asked who this fellow Maugham was anyway. Was he really important? Should they send him a guest card?

Maugham stayed at the Colonial Inn, and his choice of the Colonial increased its popularity. In 1943 the Inn gave him a sitting room at no extra cost. This he appreciated, for he couldn't afford to spend more than he had to and he found it troublesome to work in his bedroom. On fine days he spent the mornings on the beach and worked in the afternoon; on gray or foggy days he worked all day.

Maugham's presence in Edgartown in 1942 explains an unprecedented event that took place there on September 5—the world première of *The Moon and Sixpence*—at the small and shabby local movie house. Scores of celebrities came to Martha's Vineyard for the occasion, which was remarkable for another reason: Maugham made the first, and one of the very few, public speeches of his life. Stating that he hadn't known until fifteen minutes before that a speech was expected of him, he thanked those who had made the showing possible and commented briefly on the new technique employed in the film—the use of a narrator.

In a letter written a few days after the première, Maugham said that he liked Edgartown very much. He had met some pleasant people (among them Max Eastman, whom he described as "a wonderfully engaging companion"), but he didn't mention *The Moon and Sixpence.*

During the years he spent in this country, the pattern of Maugham's life remained the same. He spent the winters quietly in South Carolina. When the weather became too hot there—usually in April—he went to New York for a month or so. For many years he had stayed at the Ritz (he described it as a small family hotel), but when the Ritz couldn't give him a suite he shifted his allegiance to the Plaza and ever after went there. He was much busier in New York than elsewhere. He put in his usual three-hour stint of work, writing or correcting proof, and there was always business to attend to. He went to the theatre; during one visit he sat for a bust; he played bridge three or four nights a week; and he went out of town for several weekends.

Wherever he was, he followed the progress of the war with deep interest. Once when I was staying with him an actor called who had wangled a letter of introduction (he wanted a part in *Sheppey,* about to be produced). Maugham received him courteously. Just as he started to explain that he had nothing to do with the casting, Churchill's voice boomed over the radio. Maugham stopped in mid-sentence. For the length of the long speech there was absolute silence in the room. When Churchill had finished, Maugham turned to the flustered actor and continued where he had left off.

The war made Maugham not only more serious but more British. Before the war he was anything but the typical Britisher. The short stories in which he shows the impact of a tropical environment on the displaced Englishmen certainly do not glorify him. In fact, Maugham's fiction is full of snide remarks about his countrymen. The Dutch, the French, even the Americans in his stories show to better advantage. He was so anti-British that he planned to set up a fund in this country to help struggling young American writers.

The war changed all that. After the fall of France he became very bitter against the French. He wrote me that of the two, he thought he preferred the Italians, at that time his country's enemies. At the same time, his efforts to help England tended to make him more kindly to Britain. In his writing, "The English" became "We English." *The Hour Before the Dawn* was an all-out (and unsuccessful) attempt to portray the British sympathetically. In his essays and stories he has frequently compared the English and the French; before the war, the comparison favored the French. In the preface to *A Writer's Notebook* (1949) it strongly favors the English.

Maugham's belated love of England naturally cooled his affection for this country, or, at any rate, the material manifestation of it. He gave the manuscript of *Of Human Bondage*—sixteen leather-bound exercise books—to our Library of Congress. He said he wanted to show his appreciation of the hospitality we had extended to him, his daughter, and his two grandchildren. But England got the fund to assist struggling young writers. Maugham gave the money, but refused to decide which strugglers should be assisted. The first Somerset Maugham Award went to a young woman named A. L. Barker, who has done very well for herself since. A later award was made to the author of *Lucky Jim,* Kingsley Amis, one of England's Angry Young Men, whose work Maugham loathes.

In November, 1944, an event occurred which distressed Maugham deeply—the death of Gerald Haxton, his secretary for more than twenty-five years. *A Writer's Notebook,* published five years later, is dedicated to his memory. During the following year Maugham had no secretary. He said he couldn't afford one on the pittance his government allowed him from his earnings. Then, in December, 1945, Alan Searle, an old friend who appears as Ned Preston in "Episode" and "The Kite," came over from England to take on the job.

By the middle of the next year, having learned that the Villa Mauresque was still there, Maugham gathered up his secretary, cook, housekeeper, butler, and chauffeur and went home. He found the house in bad shape. The Italians had stolen the furniture, the Germans had drunk up the wine cellar and mined the property, and the Allies had shelled the house and planted an incendiary in the garden. Maugham gave orders for it to be put back into shape, and then betook himself to England while the work was being done. By Christmas he was back in the home he had fled from six years before and feared he might never see again.

CHAPTER 8

W. Somerset Driffield

WHEN their production slacks off, most popular writers are quickly forgotten. But at eighty-five Somerset Maugham persists not only in sticking around—artistically and financially as well as in the flesh—but year by year he gets bigger and bigger. Scarcely a week goes by that his name doesn't appear in the public prints. Somehow or other, when a large international event takes place, there he is, in the middle of it. When Grace Kelly married her prince, one of the biggest pictures in *Life* was of Maugham, and the most fascinating bit of news to come out of the wedding was that Maugham complained his feet were cold during the marriage service. *Sports Illustrated* went to Heidelberg to cover a soccer match and featured a full-page picture of Maugham kicking off the opening ball, and the caption under it was written with all the reverence of the Twenty-third Psalm.

Maugham has captured and held a huge international audience for three generations, and he has done so without the help of the critics. The intelligentsia have damned his work, yet the feeling persists that a great writer, a great artist, a towering man of letters lives on among us. How did Maugham do it?

In *Cakes and Ale,* published twenty-eight years ago, Maugham himself explained how it is done, and perhaps then he had already planned to do it. Edward Driffield, the chief character in *Cakes and Ale,* is a novelist. He is no great shakes as a writer and for most of his career the critics were mild in his praise. But he kept pegging away until eventually his years earned him reverence and the sheer bulk of his production stunned the critics. At eighty, Edward Driffield became the Grand Old Man of English Letters.

This feat puzzled Willie Ashenden, also a writer and the narrator of the novel, for like Maugham he is not prone to exaggerate the merits of a fellow author. Edward Driffield, he decided, was simply not a great writer. How could he be acclaimed one? After much thought, Willie Ashenden figured it out. Longevity did it. Longevity is genius. The real reason for the universal applause that comforts the declining years of the aged author is that intelligent people read nothing after they are thirty. "As they grow older the books they read in their youth are lit with glamour and with every year that passes they ascribe greater merit to the author who wrote them."

Driffield achieved eminence by winning over two groups, critics and readers. The cases of Driffield and Maugham are similar but not identical. Maugham's rise to grand old manhood is the more remarkable because he got there without the help of the critics, who now that he has passed eighty are kindly but not gushing.

Maugham would be less than human if he didn't revel in his belated glory, but he would be less than Maugham if he didn't wryly savor the irony of how he achieved it. There is the additional irony that it was he who, a quarter of a century before he arrived at this destination, publicly charted the way there.

By the time Maugham was acknowledged to be a Great Writer, he had almost given up being a writer. In his methodical way he gave it up type by type. He wrote his last play twenty-five years ago, the last of his four travel books two years later. About the time he left this country to return to the Mauresque, he polished off his last short story.

Few writers have ground out as many short stories as he or written them over so long a period of time, and the total is the more impressive when we bear in mind that the short story is only one of five literary types in which he trafficked. *Orientations*, his first volume of stories, was published in 1899; forty-eight years later, *Creatures of Circumstance* appeared, his last volume except for reprints. Between them there were seven other volumes. These nine contain exactly one hundred stories, almost all of which had been published in magazines before they appeared in book form. All but seven of them (the six of *Orientations* and a short short called "The Flip of a Coin") were gathered into the collected edition.

In his preface to *The World Over*, the second volume of the collected edition, Maugham says he has written nearly a hundred short stories and that *The World Over* contains all he has written except those which appear in *East and West*. The first statement is misleading and the second is untrue. He wrote more than a hundred, for many stories which appeared in magazines never found a place in any of the numerous collections.

No one knows exactly how many short stories Maugham has written—least of all Maugham, but he knows it is many more than a hundred. There are a few stories he has forgotten and many more he would like his readers to forget. Even if we had everything he wrote, it would be difficult to agree upon the total number. Fifteen of the stories which first appeared in *Ashenden* were welded into six before they were reprinted in *East and West*. A number of the sketches in *Chinese Screen* surely qualify as short stories, yet only two are included in the collected edition. It is a safe guess that the number of short stories Maugham has written is nearer a hundred and fifty than a hundred.

More remarkable than the number of Maugham's stories is their diversity in setting, mood, and character. Consider only the matter of setting. No other writer has made use of so many widely different locales: Malaya, Borneo, England, Tahiti, Mexico, Samoa, Italy, Spain, French Guiana, on shipboard, in a sanatorium, on a train, in heaven. The list could go on and on. And with the exception of heaven, not yet included in his travels, Maugham describes each place in detail. Many of the settings are of faraway places that conjure up romantic vistas in the minds of most readers, who don't therefore realize that each is realistically described. You would look long to find a misplaced flora or fauna in the whole lot of them.

But setting in Maugham's stories is more than a colorful background for plot. Setting, character, and plot are so inextricably woven together that most stories could happen only where they do. Where but in the slums of Seville would the violent action of "The Mother" be credible? Where but in the Crown Colony of Singapore would Leslie Crosbie's lawyer buy the letter which would have convicted her of the charge of murdering her lover?

When they think of Maugham's stories, many readers recall only melodramatic stories like these. In point of fact, both the melodramatic and the exotic stories are in the minority. Although he wrote too few of them, high-spirited, tongue-in-cheek tales like "The Closed Door," "Appearance and Reality," and "Mr. Harrington's Washing" are just as characteristic of him, and so are light-hearted anecdotes like "The Three Fat Women of Antibes" and "The Facts of Life."

Maugham seldom speaks at length to a group of people, but once he held his dinner guests spellbound with a description of a British ex-major whom he had encountered in India. The former officer had turned his back on the western way of life and had embraced the meditative life of the Indian fakir. Penniless and ragged, he subsisted on whatever offerings the faithful made to him. Maugham wondered what experiences could have brought about so drastic a change in his manner of living. I remarked that it sounded like good material for a short story.

"I'm afraid there isn't any story there," Maugham said. "Only a character."

This remark seems to imply that, in Maugham's opinion, a character, no matter how vivid, is not enough to make a story. Something must happen; there must be a plot. In many of his stories there is plenty of plot. "Rain," "The Outstation," "The Letter," "The Vessel of Wrath," "The Door of Opportunity," and many more have superb plots. But if by plot we mean a series of related incidents leading up to an inevitable climax, the plain fact is that many of the stories have no plot at all. There is a situation and there are vivid characters, but there is precious little story. How much story is there in "The Force of Circumstance," "Virtue," or even "The Book Bag"? There is something in them which makes excellent reading, but it isn't plot.

When he hadn't much story to tell, Maugham resorted to one of several devices. Sometimes he placed his slight story inside another, the story of how he heard the story, and this called for another setting and another character, the person who told him the story. "The Book Bag" uses this device. It not only plumps out a meager story, it also lends verisimilitude. Sometimes, as in "The Back of Beyond," Maugham devoted pages to characterizing the man to whom his story-within-a-story is told.

Another method of stretching out a story is to slow the pace and draw the characters in considerable detail. The introduction, pseudo-autobiographical material which often has only the slightest connection with what follows, may extend to two pages. In "Virtue," three pages are then devoted to characterizing Gerry Morton. The plot seems to, but doesn't really, get started when the narrator runs into Gerry in London. There follows a brief essay on the difference between people at home and abroad. Then for five pages Maugham draws the characters of Charlie and Margery Bishop. Finally, in the middle of the eleventh page of a thirty-five page story, the story gets under way with the meeting of Gerry and Margery. It halts again when Janet first comes on the scenes and Maugham makes clear what manner of female she is. But Maugham can speed up as well as slow down, and it is proof of his consummate skill that whether he is telling the story, drawing his characters, or digressing, he is never dull.

He is, as almost everyone concedes, a superb storyteller. But "superb storyteller" is a term we use loosely to describe a writer whose fiction grips our attention. The superb story may actually be very slight as a story. Maugham's greatest achievement as a fiction writer is not the stories he tells—not plot—but the characters in them. His characters are vivid, believable, and although not particularly subtle—for he is more concerned with their outer than their inner lives—remarkably individualized. They have a past as well as a present, and a life independent of the plot. They belong to and are influenced by a specific time, place, and social class. They are of many nationalities and in their actions reveal their national characteristics: the highborn Spaniard's pride, the Frenchwoman's common sense, the German's sentimentality, the Englishman's consciousness of class. The few Americans in Maugham's novels and short stories lay bare their essential Americanism by saying "Gee" at frequent intervals.

When a writer has drawn thousands of characters it is inevitable that some will resemble others. There are a few stock characters in Maugham's fiction and some repeats. Isabel Longstaffe is a younger version of the self-assured, bloodsucking Mrs. Barton Travers. Mrs. Driffield is a more carefully drawn Mrs. Strickland. Warburton, Ferdy Rabenstein, and Elliott Templeton are sisters under the skin, and cousins of the non-fictional Augustus Hare. But the repeats are few.

Maugham's relation to his characters is one of the distinctive qualities of his fiction. He never merges his personality with theirs. In fact, he holds himself as aloof from them as he does from his friends. He analyzes them impersonally; he is tolerant of their humanity and sorrowed by their self-deception. His pity is God-like in its remoteness from the weakness which arouses it. That is why we understand his characters but seldom enter into their feelings.

After he gave up short story writing, Maugham continued to write novels. Two more round out the list of twenty he wrote. (He prefers to be remembered as the author of only thirteen of them.) He planned to write one more, and he made notes for it. Its setting was to be the London slums, and it would have pleased Maugham to end his career with a novel employing the same setting as his first. It's as well he didn't write it.

Then and Now, the second from last, is like the second a historical novel. It is more history than novel. The narrative is a slight anecdote better suited to short story than novel length. The setting of Italy at the beginning of the sixteenth century allowed Maugham to bring in two examples of one of his favorite character types: Machiavelli, a young rogue on the make; and Caesar Borgia, a master rogue at the height of his power.

When he had just about completed the novel Maugham told me that he planned to call it "Conversation Piece," a more apt title than *Then and Now*, for the book is little more than a series of static scenes and conversations. But he changed his mind when I reminded him that Noel Coward had pre-empted that title.

Catalina, Maugham's last novel, he completed on his seventy-third birthday, exactly fifty years after the publication of his first novel. He had had the story in mind for some forty years but hadn't got around to writing it before. *Catalina* is short, charming, and unpretentious, far more entertaining than its ambitious predecessor, even though, in order to provide three dollars' worth, Maugham dragged it out some seventy pages beyond its logical stopping place.

Maugham is still writing one kind of prose—criticism—and no doubt will continue to do so until he dies. He has been writing daily for sixty-five years and is too old to mend his ways. Moreover, criticism increases his stature as a serious writer. Yet in his British way he has always belittled his pretensions as a critic and has been careful to dissociate himself from two other kinds of critic: the professionals, a breed he has no love for, and the professors of literature, who write books so that their merits as teachers will be recognized and rewarded.

In the preface to *Books and You*, Maugham says that he

writes his little book not as a critic but as a plain man with a proper interest in humanity. That is nonsense. What else but a critic is the author of *Books and You?* As Maugham well knows, plain men with a proper—or improper—interest in humanity don't write books, or at any rate seldom get them published. What Maugham wants to imply is that as a critic he is off his beat and has produced very little.

Therefore you are quite surprised when you gather it together to find that Maugham has produced quite a lot of criticism. In addition to whole books (*The Vagrant Mood, Great Novelists and Their Novels, Books and You,* and another volume soon to appear), there are chunks of criticism in *Don Fernando* and *The Gentleman in the Parlour. The Summing Up* is a collection of critical essays. The introductions to his many collections would fill a volume, and should. In fact, Maugham's published criticism bulks larger than that of many professional critics.

Maugham brings valuable equipment to the practice of criticism: common sense, a vast knowledge of human nature and the writer's craft, and his own skill as a writer. When he is analyzing the work of an individual, his approach is usually through the biography of his subject. He likes to explain the significance of facts which biographers have recorded but, he thinks, misinterpreted, like Jane Austen's failure to write for eleven years or Melville's transformation from an apparently normal young man into the pessimist who wrote *Pierre.* Yet for those who would study his work in similar fashion Maugham has set up a roadblock by his refusal to sanction the writing of his own life. Perhaps some future critic could draw significant inferences from his passion for bridge or travel, for example, if a biographer were allowed to record these facts for posterity.

Like his fiction, Maugham's criticism varies in quality. The best is remarkably good, for instance his analyses of the short stories of Chekov and Maupassant. Much of his criticism is a thinly disguised justification of his own practice as a writer, but it suffers remarkably little from this, for Maugham is never silly, angry, or contentious. The poorest, in my opinion, is that which appears in the prefaces to Maugham's selection of the world's ten greatest novels. (These prefaces were later published in a volume called *Great Novelists and Their Novels,* and then, enlarged, as *The Art of Fiction.*) Maugham is a man of many ideas, but by the time he wrote these critical introductions he had expressed all of them, and some of them many times. But perhaps it is unfair to decry his repetitiousness. If it is a fault, it is one apparent only to critics and others who read too much. For the reader who comes across these ideas for the first time in this work, it is irrelevant that Maugham has said it all many times before, for he still has the knack of saying it gracefully.

Life at the Villa Mauresque today is not quite so grand as it was in 1939. Now there are only two gardens—one for winter, one for summer flowers—and the pre-war staff of thirteen has been cut to five. Maugham does not complain. With a cook and two footmen he can still put out an adequate meal when his old friend Winston Churchill drops in for lunch. The statue of Kuan Yin, the Chinese goddess of grace, still decorates the marble entrance hall, and here and there are paintings by Renoir, Degas, and Picasso. The Gauguin which he brought back from Tahiti once more refreshes his spirit when he goes to his writing room each morning. In his bedroom he can rest on a cushion specially embroidered by Marie Laurencin and look at a volume of drawings which Matisse gave him. High up on the hill beside his house the water still gushes through the marble mask by Bernini into the blue-tiled swimming pool.

Nowadays Maugham prefers to live simply. He is getting old and feels it, house guests tire him and interfere with his work, and it isn't worth the effort to run a free Hotel Splendide for his friends. And with all the money in the world it wouldn't be as easy to do so as it was before the war, for times have changed on the Riviera too. Like everyone else who has servants, Maugham has a servant problem. In fact, he has thought of selling the Mauresque and moving to Italy. But he is a stubborn man; he has long planned to die in his painted bed in his bedroom overlooking the Mediterranean, and it will annoy him to die anywhere else.

He takes the chance of doing so, for he continues to travel. He drives to Spain in the spring to spend some of the royalties that accumulate there; he goes frequently to England; after an absence of sixty-five years he recently returned to Heidelberg, where the University gave a dinner in his honor and the students organized a beer-drinking bout. He has made several last visits to this country. In fact, whenever he sees a ship, he itches to get on it, and often does.

Everywhere he goes these days, honors are heaped upon him. It was not always so. When he went to India in 1937 to gather material for *The Razor's Edge*, the Indians were friendly and helpful as soon as they learned he hadn't come to sell something or to shoot tigers. But although he was known the world over at the time, the British colony high-hatted him. They did warm up a bit when they learned that he had a socially acceptable brother— Viscount Maugham, then Lord Chancellor of England— and on the strength of that he got a few invitations to lunch.

Maugham does not tell us why he was high-hatted, but the reasons are clear. In his stories he has not been over kind to British colonials. A more important reason is the gossip that Maugham has stayed with people as their guest and then caricatured them in fiction. I have been told this repeatedly by people who claim to know the people who entertained him, but I have never been able to find out who the people are or what monsters he turned them into. It is the kind of inside information people love to show they know. The gossip is so persistent that Maugham tried, without success, to quash it in *The Summing Up*. He said he was not, he supposed, the only writer thus maligned and stated positively that he had never even met certain people who claim he has treated them con- tumeliously.

I believe him. Assuming that Maugham is heel enough to

act as gossip says he has, it would not suit his purposes as a writer to do so. It is seldom that a writer draws a character wholly from life, for such a character would not be convincing. As Maugham explains, the writer of fiction takes a hint here and there from the living model and through his knowledge of human nature builds up a plausible whole. Maugham has of course used living models, but he has almost always changed them beyond recognition. (The exception, of course, is Hugh Walpole.) I know two persons who modeled for him, but I should never have known this from the stories in which they appear. I know it because Maugham told me. The gossip persists not because it has any foundation but because people give themselves a specious importance by claiming they have entertained Maugham and then been given the dirty end of the stick. It is unlikely to die down until both Maugham and his phantom hosts are in their graves.

Maugham, however, is in no hurry to die. Most of his energies today are devoted to postponing that event. But he is not the man to ignore his advanced age. Indeed, he has wangled an extraordinary amount of publicity out of that ordinary fact. When he reached seventy he described himself as an Old Party; at seventy-five he became a Very Old Party; and in every interview since he has made ostentatious reference to his age. His secret ambition, some of his friends say, is to live longer than Shaw lived, but he is unwilling to subsist on lettuce and celery in order to do so. When he was seriously ill a couple of years ago, his doctor advised him to give up cigarettes for three months. After that, he was told, he wouldn't want

them. Maugham did as he was bid, but three months to
the day, he lit up a cigarette and he has been lighting
them up ever since. He says that at his age it is absurd to
give up any pleasure; not many remain, and one should
enjoy them all.

Shortly after he returned to the Mauresque, the Old
Party began a series of last voyages. In January, 1949, in
order to keep a promise he had made a quarter of a
century before, he journeyed to San Francisco to spend
his seventy-fifth birthday with Bertram Alanson, an old
friend to whom he had dedicated *The Trembling of a
Leaf* twenty-eight years before. The next year he was in
this country again, this time to attend the première of
Trio, a package movie of three of his short stories. (He
is one of three writers credited with the script.) Two years
before *Trio, Quartet,* a similar package, had appeared,
and a year later these were followed by *Encore.* Maugham
told me that the problem in selecting the ten stories that
make up the three movies was to find those which couldn't
possibly offend anybody. In order to render one of the
stories ("Mr. Know-All") inoffensive it was apparently
necessary to make it pointless. Any suggestion that Mr.
Know-All is Jewish was scrupulously avoided in the film,
although as everybody knows who has read the original
story, Mr. Know-All proves to be the hero. "The Alien
Corn," one of the stories that make up *Quartet,* was put
through the same laundry.

During this visit Maugham participated in a TV series
called "The Somerset Maugham Theater," based on more
of his short stories. He also attended a party given by his

TV sponsors at the Stork Club, where he shocked the other guests by drinking Ovaltine. *Life* magazine, which had managed to show up wherever he was living—France, South Carolina, Edgartown, New York—spent another day with him. It could hardly be called a typical day, for during it Maugham bought a Renoir painting entitled "Three Sisters," but it included typical activities: he shopped for seeds at Max Schling's, at Gristede's he ordered quantities of food to be sent to the Mauresque, and he spent the evening playing bridge with Elsa Maxwell.

In 1952 he made a last voyage to Athens and Istanbul, and the first of several last visits to Spain. Nineteen fifty-four was a big year. On January 25, Willie Maugham was eighty years old, and all the world took notice. He went to London for the event, and was made much of. Even royalty yielded to him: *London Calling* put his picture on its cover and the story of the royal tour inside. *Punch* printed an affectionate caricature of him and a bad poem about him. Newspapers and magazines on this side of the Atlantic also gave the story a big play. The *New York Times* published a long article, and *Clinical Excerpts* summarized his career with particular attention to his diseases and his training at St. Thomas' Hospital. Its photograph of Dr. Maugham, M.R.C.S., L.R.C.P., was taken some fifty years before.

More honors were ahead. Maugham had long worn the rosette of the French Legion of Honour, but his own country had cast a cold eye on an Englishman who chose to live away from England and who viewed his countrymen with such ironic detachment. Now, mindful of his war work and jogged no doubt by the eightieth birthday celebration, England acknowledged Maugham's belated courtship of her. On June 9, along with 2499 others (including Edith Sitwell) he was named in Queen Elizabeth's birthday honors list. Maugham's recognition was no mere knighthood. He was named Companion of Honor and thus joined a select company which includes Winston Churchill and is limited to sixty-five. For his investiture he shrugged off the pain of a broken rib, donned his top hat, and made his way to Buckingham Palace. Newspapers around the world reported the event.

His years haven't slowed Maugham's pace noticeably. In 1955 he attended a film festival in Germany; then he went to England. After that he joined his old friend the Aga Khan in Egypt for a fortnight's visit on a houseboat on the Nile. Each July he goes to Austria's Bad Gastein for his cure.

When he is at the Mauresque he accepts the homage of a stream of old friends who drop in to see him: Churchill, the Windsors, Ilka Chase, and many more. Ilka came over when she was in the neighborhood to cover the Rainier wedding. In deference to his years and fame she now calls him Mr. Willie. She thinks it is a little tactless of him to be so spry at his age. Showing her around the rebuilt Mauresque, he sprinted up the formidable staircase and gazed with waspish satisfaction at her puffing at his heels. He pointed carelessly to a pile of invitations from the palace at Monaco and grumbled at having to put on a stiff shirt to accept them, but Ilka thought he was pleased to be included in the festivities. After all, he must have remembered what happened to Elliott Templeton when he was an old man. Mr. Willie's wedding present to the Grimaldis was three handsomely bound volumes of his short stories. "Less expensive for me than a jewel and more valuable to them," he remarked.

Last year Maugham popped into the news with a request that was reported all over the English-speaking world. He had already refused to help a number of people who wanted to write his biography. Now, through the London *Daily Mail*, he asked all those who have any letters written by him to burn them. He had, he said, instructed his literary executor to destroy all private papers and forever forbid the publication of his letters. He added that these were his personal affair and he could not see that a public airing would serve any useful purpose.

This is a strange point of view for one whose criticism of fellow writers has involved extensive use of their letters and biography. No one knows better than Maugham that the study of a writer's life provides an understanding of his work, and no one wants his work understood more than he.

Public reaction to this unusual request was mostly surprise. Even his brother the Viscount seemed startled. Willie hadn't asked him to destroy his letters, he said. One magazine commented on the request under the heading "The Letters Are for Burning." The Chicago *Sun-Times*, in an editorial, remarked acidly that a man who has spent a lifetime prying into the affairs of humankind doesn't want his own affairs pried into, and that a man like Maugham, who has been very much of a public figure for sixty years, ought to know better.

Maugham's request would seem to be an elderly indiscretion, for it has not had the desired effect and has given the letters a specious value. It is unlikely that anyone who has a Maugham letter has obliged. Asked by the *Daily Mail* whether Maugham feared any early love letters coming to light, Alan Searle replied stiffly, "I can assure you that there is nothing of that sort at all."

It is most unlikely that there is. Maugham is too shrewd and discreet a person ever to have put on paper anything that would seriously embarrass him if it were made public. Many of his letters, like anybody else's, are of no particular interest—an invitation to dinner, thanks for the socks or the ham sent him, remarks on the war and the weather and the book he has just read. Readers might find a few of these letters mildly interesting but hardly titillating. The letters are not even malicious, for Maugham reserved his malice for his published work. But some letters contain facts of great value to anyone who undertakes a serious study of his work: what he is working on, problems which have come up in connection with it, books he needs to consult, future writing plans.

But perhaps Maugham's odd request is not so ill-advised as it seems; perhaps at eighty-three he could still figure all the angles. His motive for forbidding the publication of his letters may have been to preserve the public image of himself that has served him so well, that of a cynical, mysterious, and slightly sinister being. This he is not in his letters, and so he would like them destroyed. His

letters show quite another side of him. They would dis-
appoint his public, and doubly so now that his edict has
whetted curiosity.

When the critics of the future make up their minds
about him, what will be Maugham's rating in the world
of letters? Will he be a good writer of the second rank or
will he become a footnote in the histories of literature?
His present equivocal position supplies little clue to the
answer. He has great prestige but no solid reputation. He
is enormously popular with all kinds of readers, but they
like him for different reasons. He is the lowbrow's Proust
and the highbrow's Mickey Spillane. Few but the un-
critical wholeheartedly praise his fiction. The others have
reservations. The intelligentsia, perhaps displeased that
they enjoy what their critical sense does not wholly approve of, speak contemptuously of it.

Maugham has been around for so long that the critics
have pretty well made up their minds about him and tend
to repeat their judgments. For example, they call his
stories melodramatic. There is violence aplenty in the
background of Maugham's stories, but his fondness for
melodrama has been exaggerated. He usually eschews the
melodramatic scene. The lurid and the sensational in his
stories generally take place offstage. We never see the
Reverend Mr. Davidson make a pass at Sadie nor glimpse
her horror when she gathers what he is up to. We do not
witness the sister's suicide in "The Book Bag" nor are we
present when the wife discovers the incestuous relationship between brother and sister. In the short story "The

Letter" there is no scene between Leslie and the lover who discarded her: when the story opens, Leslie is in jail for his murder.

Maugham has, in fact, fared badly at the hands of the critics. Individual books have been widely, and of recent years respectfully, reviewed, but when they write their own books, the critics pass over him. Maugham noted the fact that only two major critics have written appreciatively of the whole body of his work. Most of the reviews have been patronizing. He has repeatedly been damned with the faint praise of "competent," a word that infuriates him, especially as it was he who first characterized himself thus.

Publicly Maugham professes to find this neglect perfectly natural. He says the critics have ignored him because he didn't write the currently popular propaganda novels and because his literary models and his technique were old-fashioned. This is not the whole story, if it is any part of it.

Ironically, two of Maugham's greatest achievements as a writer explain in part the low esteem in which the critics hold him. One is his mastery of technique. It is no virtue to know how to tell a story if the story you have to tell is trivial. Maugham's skill was too often employed to produce a novel like *The Painted Veil*. When, despite superior craftsmanship, the finished product is second-rate, a writer's skill becomes a strike against him.

Maugham's other achievement which ran him afoul of the critics is that he wrote one superlative novel and never again reached that level. The critics want to know why. Did he sell out to Mammon? Malcolm Cowley thinks that success cut Maugham off from the circles that gave him his best material—which, as Cowley points out, is Maugham's explanation for the failure of Arnold Bennett's later novels. My opinion is that Maugham couldn't write another *Of Human Bondage* because there is no warmth in the man he made himself into. He could no longer identify with a character like Philip Carey. After *Of Human Bondage* he stood aside and observed his fellow beings with that faint hostility which he calls tolerance.

What has chiefly annoyed the critics about Maugham is that he is not someone else. They wanted him to be a better and a different kind of writer. That was not possible. He wrote as well as he could and he wrote the only kind of story he was able to write. And he was lucky. Talent, will power, and luck combined to produce the richest harvest he was capable of. He will go to his grave an emptied vessel.

What the critics of the future will say is anybody's guess. I will venture to suggest that Maugham will be rated higher than he is now. He has not been overpraised during his life and therefore need not suffer the inevitable depreciation which is the fate of those who have. He is, in my opinion, a good writer of the second rank.

What are the limitations that prevent his being first rank? One is that as a storyteller he is too exclusively concerned with outer action, the clash between persons, and too little concerned with the drama of the mind. The *effect* of Philip Carey's passion for Mildred Rogers is vividly depicted; the explanation of it is hardly hinted at. We get no glimpse of Davidson's titanic inner struggle; "Rain" is the story of what he did as a consequence of it and how it affected others. Maugham would have us believe that to tell an entertaining story a writer must concentrate on external action. But the stories of such writers as Katherine Mansfield, Sherwood Anderson, and James Gould Cozzens prove that a writer can be just as entertaining who concerns himself largely with the inner life of his characters.

Another strike against Maugham is that to achieve his dramatic effects he used a formula. Maugham is annoyed when people speak of his "formula," but it can only be the word he objects to. Perhaps in its harshest sense it is unfair. The formula writer ignores many facts he is aware of and bends others into a pattern which experience has taught him is effective. Maugham's formula does not ignore facts he is aware of. It does no violence to his deepest convictions. It simply milks these of their dramatic potentialities, and since he is a writer and not a philosopher, this is not surprising. One Maugham conviction with limitless dramatic possibilities is that man is in bondage to his passions; these and his environment determine his actions, and his will is powerless against them. Other cherished notions are that man is a bundle of contradictions and given time will reveal himself to be the opposite of what he seems; that there are hidden possibilities of savagery in the most respectable of women. These and other convictions Maugham has dramatized so often that from the critic's point of view they constitute a formula.

W. SOMERSET MAUGHAM

Maugham fails to achieve top rank also because of his narrow range and lack of development as a thinker. His craftsmanship improved but his view of life remained what it was at twenty-five. The ideas that inform his fiction are few, and the important ones are all there in *Mrs. Craddock*, one of his earliest novels. Successive novels merely ring changes on them.

What, then, are Maugham's merits that entitle him to second rank? Once he said to me that the most valuable quality a work of fiction can have is readability. Many good, even great, novels do not have it, he said; some poor ones do. It compensates for many obvious faults. It is shared by writers as different from each other as Dickens and Jane Austen. It is an elusive quality which keeps the reader turning the pages with delighted anticipation.

It seems to me that Maugham's work has this quality of readability. Of course any popular novelist is found readable by thousands or he doesn't become popular. But most novelists as popular as Maugham find their readers among the intellectual middle or lower classes; Maugham's readers belong to all intellectual classes. However they disparage him, those who read Kafka also read Maugham, and most of those who buy Cronin or Ferber have read *Of Human Bondage*. It is no small accomplishment to have written books that attract so diverse a group of readers.

Another merit is a quality in Maugham which is reflected in his writing and which will in time earn him the respect so far denied him—complete, almost fantastic integrity. With intelligence, an open mind, and trained powers of observation he has tried to see life steadily and see it as a whole. The mature Maugham never poses, he never pretends to be what he isn't, he accepts no second-hand judgments. As Richard Aldington puts it, "He refuses to conform to anybody's idea of what is right to think and feel and do and has labored with the utmost sincerity to discover what he really does think and feel." That is why readers who indignantly reject his view of life nevertheless find engrossing the stories pervaded by it.

In this late autumn of his life Maugham spends most of his days at the Villa Mauresque. He likes to sit in the sun and look at the blue Mediterranean below. Now, within hailing distance of death, having had all the good things in this life that money can buy, he would like two more that money can't buy. One he speaks of freely; the other he would be embarrassed to have you mention.

He wants many more years in this world. When he was eighty-three, a reporter asked him cheekily whether he had any future plans. Maugham replied crustily, "Yes. Definitely. To live on." On his eighty-fourth birthday he said wistfully, "If you are small, Death may quite likely overlook you."

More than life, Maugham wants recognition of his merits as a writer. He makes no exalted claim; in fact, he can't quite convince himself that his detractors aren't right. He would like some wholehearted support from the critics.

He has always asked questions and sought answers, but he has not found satisfactory answers to two questions of burning interest to him. If he gets an answer to the first, we shall never know it. And when we get the answer to the second, it will be too late for him to know it.

Is there a hereafter or does this world terminate our existence? Maugham's rational mind has concluded there is no life after this one, but his heart remains unconvinced.

Still, annihilation of self is tolerable if one leaves behind something of enduring value. What, he would like to know, will be his ultimate place in the literature of England?

Index

Mayfair, 55, 65
Mediterranean Pilot, 161
Mei-tan-fu, China, 87
Melville, Herman, 198
Mencken, H. L., 71, 121
Meredith, George, 94
Middlemarch, G. Eliot, 77
Ming Dynasty, 86
"Miss Thompson," 71–74
"Mr. Harrington's Washing," 193
Molière, 56
Monaco, 205
Moon and Sixpence, The, 39, 68–70, 76, 79, 81, 84, 93, 112, 184
Mordaunt, Elinor, 97
Morton, Gerry, 194, 195
"Mother, The," 193
My South Sea Island, 129

Narrator, Maugham's use of in fiction, 85, 86, 99–102, 149, 182
Narrow Corner, The, 139–143
Nazism, 149
New York, 20, 23, 55, 56, 57, 72, 133, 151, 168, 172, 177, 184, 185
New Yorker magazine, 123
New York Times, 204
Nice, 152, 157, 160, 166, 167
Nichols, Captain, 70
Norah, 61
Notebooks, Maugham's, 38, 83
see also Writer's Notebook, A

Of Human Bondage, 28, 29, 31, 37, 41, 43, 47, 58–63, 68, 75, 100, 148, 149, 186, 210, 212
characterization in, 60, 61
material for, 48
Maugham's opinion of, 59
movie of, 16
philosophy of, 62
popularity of, 59

publication of, 58
writing of, 58
O'Hara, John, 145
On a Chinese Screen, 83–85, 140, 192
Orientations, 44, 191
Our Betters, 57, 65, 66, 165
"Outstation, The," 194

Pago Pago, 70, 71
Painted Veil, The, 86, 89, 140, 209
Paravicini, Vincent, 64, 151
Paravicini, Mrs. Vincent, *see* Maugham, Liza
Paris, 25, 27, 45–48, 51, 149–151, 163
Parker, Dorothy, 126
Parker's, 171–177, 179, 180
Pearson's magazine, 136
Penelope, 55, 57
Petrograd, 67
Pfeiffer, Karl George; acquaintance with Maugham, 17, 22, 23, 75–77
Picasso, Pablo, 200
Pierre, Melville, 198
Plaza Hotel, New York, 177, 185
Plot, in Maugham's fiction, 194, 195
Power, Tyrone, 183
Preston, Ned, 187
Price, Fanny, 61
Protestantism, 90
Proust, Marcel, 208
Pseudonym Library, 35
Punch, 50, 204

Quartet, 179, 203
Queen Elizabeth's birthday honors list, 205

Rabenstein, Ferdy, 196
Rain, 71, 72, 89, 194, 211
Rainier, Prince, 189, 205
Rand, Sally, 73
Randolph, Clemence, 71, 74

INDEX